MINORITY RULES

MINORITY RULES

Turn Your Ethnicity into
a Competitive Edge

KENNETH ARROYO ROLDAN
AND GARY M. STERN

Collins
An Imprint of HarperCollinsPublishers

HarperCollins books may be purchased for educational, business, or sales
promotional use. For information, please write to: Special Markets Department, HarperCollins Publishers, 10 East 53rd Street, New York, NY
10022.

Designed by Ellen Cipriano

Library of Congress Cataloging-in-Publication Data has been applied for.

ISBN-10: 0-06-085205-4
ISBN-13: 978-0-06-085205-4

06 07 08 09 10 DIX/RRD 10 9 8 7 6 5 4 3 2 1

To the following people at various corporations who were instrumental in sharing their career blueprints, thank you. Without their success stories, this book would not be as thorough: Tony Brown, Robert D. Charles, Bruce Colligan, Bill Davis, Jerri DeVard, Dave Edwards, Berlinda Fontenot-Jamerson, Kirk Forrest, Anthony W. Gilliard, Carlos Gutierrez, Deborah Helmer, Sheila Lewis, Carlos Linares, Cheryl McCants, Rob McCowan, Paulette Mullings, Luis Nunez, Cynthia Park, Monica Pool Ross, Stephanie Royster, Connie Simons, Lisa Skriloff, Kevin Stephens, Johnny Taylor, Amy Titus, Carlos Valle, Mary A. Winston, Melvin Young, and Al Zollar.

A special thanks to Wesley Poriotis, chairman and founder of Wesley, Brown & Bartle, for providing me with the opportunity to understand the intricacies of executive search and the challenges people of color face in corporate America, and for the opportunity to sustain his legacy. A warm thanks to my partners, Barbara Mendez Tucker and Jeff Greene, who continually encouraged me to broaden my horizons, and to the entire WB&B team for their support.

I'd also like to thank two people who contributed to making this book happen: our agent, Linda Konner, who helped shape the book; and our editor, Leah Spiro, for her keen eye and business acumen.

To my wife, Magdalen, and my children, Hamilton and Juliana, and my mom, Carmen, and in memory of my mother-in-law, Ellen, for their love and inspiration.

And from co-writer Gary Stern, thanks to my wife, Judith Frey, for always being there and offering support.

"Ultimately, America's answer to the intolerant man is diversity, the very diversity which our heritage of religious freedom has inspired."
—*Robert F. Kennedy*

CONTENTS

FOREWORD

by Kenneth Arroyo Roldan

■

If you're a person of color or a woman and want to move up the corporate ladder, you won't find a strategic career blueprint or helpful tips directly targeted to you in any textbook. And while an MBA program can teach you about profit and loss, running a business, and acquisition and growth strategies, you won't learn how to break through the glass ceiling and granite walls. Textbooks and MBA programs are too formal and academic to teach you the nitty-gritty details of how to select a mentor, understand the politics of what makes a corporation tick, overcome the fact that you haven't been raised in a privileged environment, and master networking effectively, especially outside your own ethnic group.

In my experience as an attorney specializing in employment discrimination cases and as the CEO of one of the country's leading executive search firms with a specialized practice in diversity recruitment, I've seen the obstacles that corporations place in the way of minority advancement. I've observed the patterns that minorities fall into that prevent their gaining entrance into the power positions of corporations.

I wrote *Minority Rules: Turn Your Ethnicity into a Competitive Edge* to provide minority professionals with the skills and know-how to overcome and surmount the obstacles to career advancement. Minority readers will change their outlook about what it takes to advance and build a career in the corporate or nonprofit business workplace. This book provides a much-needed road map to success: how to plan your career from the day you begin at a corporation and map out a strategy to advance your career to the very top. Nothing should stand in the way of your performance carrying you through the corporation to reach your natural potential.

I understand that it's tough for anyone to advance in the corporate world. As the employee rises up the corporate ladder, the number of executive positions dwindles. Moving up takes a combination of skills: hard work, persistence, networking, and knowing the right people. But for women and people of color, it's much tougher than it is for majority candidates. That's why *Minority Rules* has been written: to provide minorities with insights into how the corporate world really works, and with strategies for replicating and overcoming the social connections of their white counterparts.

Why am I the right person to write this book? As the songwriter Joni Mitchell said, I've seen life from both sides now. As a former civil prosecutor enforcing laws that protect women and people of color, I've witnessed the effects of businesses' shutting out, denying, and squelching the careers of talented individuals. As the CEO of an executive recruiting firm that has placed minorities in the executive suites of the most powerful corporations in the world, I've been on the front lines of educating corporate America and helping minority candidates succeed. Despite equal-opportunity and antidiscrimination laws, I've seen the great disparity between the good intentions of companies and their actual hiring practices. To this day, most companies still give only lip service to diversity programs and initiatives, as evidenced by the paltry number of senior executives of color within the Fortune 500. Even companies named to the list of Top 50 Companies for Diversity in the United States have done an abysmal job of promoting minorities from the mid-management level up to the board of directors.

As a consultant and recruiter for these companies, I understand what makes Fortune 500 companies tick. When advising future executives, I don't have to be politically correct, don't have to sugarcoat the message or conceal the realities of what it takes to advance in a given company. I can call a diversity committee a charade if it doesn't lead to hiring more minority executives. I can also critique minority candidates when they either think too highly of themselves or are oblivious of the cues that corporations send out that, if followed, would help them enormously.

The time for this book is now. We have a political climate that shuns affirmative action and believes in entrepreneurship, capitalism, and letting market forces produce winners and losers. This book isn't about how affirmative action will help you overcome hurdles; instead, it proposes that the key to advancement is your own performance. It's your performance that counts. Just as in baseball, our national pastime, where .325 hitters and 40-home-run batters get the bigger contracts, performance is what will separate you from your peers.

A little historical perspective can be helpful in understanding the underpinnings of this book. In its influential "Workforce 2000" study, the Hudson Institute, a think tank that specializes in social policy issues, opened our eyes by documenting how, during the 1990s the minority population was becoming the majority because of changing demographics due to immigration, heightened birthrates, and an exploding Latino population. Companies that ignore hiring and promoting a diverse slate of employees run the risk of losing touch with their customers and eroding their global market share. Many companies took notice. They hired diversity directors, funded special diversity programs aimed at sensitizing their staff to dealing with minorities, and felt much better about their efforts.

But what they didn't do was to create a succession plan that provided upward career mobility for a diverse group of high performers. Nor did many minority employees step up to understand the inner, political workings of a corporation, or identify a "godfather" who would serve as their mentor, or challenge themselves on the job to expand their responsibilities into profit and loss areas, and to network, network, network.

Even well-publicized lawsuits did not encourage companies into opening the executive doors to minorities. When Texaco Corporation and Mitsubishi Motors were found guilty of discrimination in two separate cases in 1996, their reputations suffered temporary damage. But nearly ten years later, their corporate offices are filled with white men and little has changed within their executive suites. Hence, minorities cannot depend on affirmative-action programs or class-action suits to change things.

Nor have protest movements by leading minority figures resulted in substantive change either. The Reverend Jesse Jackson's Rainbow PUSH/Wall Street Project has earned reams of publicity, but what concrete changes have resulted from its efforts to change the composition of executives at the top of the corporate food chain? Little has changed, while PUSH has accepted corporate dollars and provided a diversion rather than achieving true change in power positions at the upper levels of management. After eight years of organizing efforts around Wall Street, there have been minimal, if any, changes in the board levels and executive suites, despite the fact that Jackson's organization has raised millions of dollars from financial-services, insurance, and other companies. Funds may go into education, but his project is not leading to the sweeping changes at the middle to senior levels that would signify minority advancement.

Though I haven't been involved in formal protests, I've been on the front line of trying to place minorities into senior positions at Fortune 500 companies. I too had to make the long climb to enter these corridors of powers. Born to a Puerto Rican mother and abandoned by my father at an early age, I was raised in the tough streets of New York City. Attending a public high school in Queens, New York, I became quite skilled at assimilating into a variety of ethnic groups. I learned how to deal with whites, African Americans, Caribbeans, Cubans, and people from other ethnic groups—a useful skill for a career in executive recruiting. I was one of the few Hispanics in a special international baccalaureate program in my high school, but faced no discrimination until I met with my guidance counselor. I had top grades and wanted to apply to several Ivy League schools, but my guidance counselor (whose name I will never forget but will spare you) said, "Ken, despite your good grades, you're not Ivy League material. You'll never get in." But he never explained why good grades and extracurricular activities wouldn't lead to acceptance for me. I presumed he figured that Ivy League schools would never admit a Latino kid, bright or not. Undeterred, I applied to and got into Cornell University. It was my first lesson on how to overcome obstacles, how not to listen to those who think that people of color can't accomplish what anyone else can.

Graduating from Cornell with a degree in microbiology, I changed directions and became interested in law. I gained a paralegal degree from Adelphi University, and was hired as a paralegal at Reichenbaum & Silberstein (currently known as Silberstein, Awad & Miklos), a Long Island negligence and medical malpractice firm, where partners Joseph Awad and Joseph Miklos served as my mentors. They gave me the opportunity to sit in during a major medical malpractice trial, and as a result, I fell in love with law. I continued to work there as a paralegal while attending Touro Law Center, where I earned my law degree. After working at the Northern Manhattan Coalition for Immigrant Rights, a nonprofit organization providing education to the Latino community, I became an Assistant Attorney General at the Office of the New York State Attorney General, specializing in employment discrimination cases. I saw firsthand how companies discriminated against women and people of color. That experience had a profound impact on my career and influenced me to want to help corporations do the right thing.

I loved law but found myself becoming complacent in the Attorney General's office. After an informal introduction to Wesley, Brown & Bartle, a leading executive search firm, Wesley Poriotis, the company's founder, took me under his wing. Interested in pursuing my own entrepreneurial tendencies, I joined the firm. At the firm, the harder you work, and the more you problem solve, the more income you can generate, just as in corporate life. I could tap my attorney's research skills, and my upbringing, which showed me how to get along with people of all ethnic backgrounds. As a recruiter, I learned how to master various industries, including aerospace and defense, retail, financial services, oil and energy, and manufacturing. I learned a critical lesson that is the guiding philosophy of this book: Companies, for the most part, aren't racist or discriminatory. But they don't have the infrastructure or skills to support minorities and to promote them. As CEO, I work with companies to overcome their limitations, just as I'm trying to help *you,* the readers of this book, surmount obstacles.

I've learned that high-performing, ambitious minority professionals must depend on themselves and have a sense of entitlement. The onus is on us (excuse the pun) to figure out how to overcome the barriers that prevent us from reaching the executive suite. In *Minor-*

ity Rules: Turn Your Ethnicity into a Competitive Edge, I provide a step-by-step strategic road map on how to surmount these barriers and build a case so strong that companies have no choice but to promote you. But this will take hard work, fortitude beyond what most humans can display, and perseverance like that of Edmund Hillary, the first climber to reach the apex of Mount Everest. But if you take my advice, identify the right mentor, learn how to play corporate politics, truly understand the corporation's culture, and learn how to read the corporate tea leaves, you'll give yourself your best shot at achieving your dream and becoming the senior vice president, and beyond.

This is the land of opportunity. But too many minorities want instant recognition that will enable them to ascend in the corporation. There are no magic bullets. For Carlos Gutierrez, who rose from cereal salesman to CEO of Kellogg's (at one time the only Latino CEO of a Fortune 500 company) and commerce secretary under President George W. Bush, it took hard work, and providing challenges for him, and keeping his eye on that next rung. That's what *Minority Rules* is all about: laying the groundwork (and much more) for reaching your career potential.

MINORITY RULES

THE OVERVIEW:
MINORITY RULES: TURN YOUR ETHNICITY
INTO A COMPETITIVE EDGE

■

Introduction: Developing a
Strategic Career Road Map—Creating
Your Own Personal Success Plan

SUCCESS AT A corporation doesn't happen by itself. It's not created by spontaneous combustion; it's planned, focused, and targeted. For minority employees, who face stiff competition from their majority counterparts who may be better connected and hail from the right schools, it means overcoming all of the hurdles that come with growing up African American, Latino, Asian, female, and "different" in the United States. Our opening chapter lays the groundwork for the six steps that can be used to develop a strategic career road map. Having a sense of where you want to go and what you have to do to get there will help you advance to the next rung, and the next rung after that. Creating a strategic blueprint, mapping out as best you can where you'd like to be in five years, in ten years, will point you in the right direction. In this chapter we discuss researching companies to make sure you start at a company where minorities are treated with respect, understanding the unwritten code of corporations, mastering core competencies, and recognizing how the relationships you form in your early years can take you far up the corporate ladder. Success is a matter of design, based on your performance and character, and derived from having a sense of purpose.

Chapter 1: Building Your Career Step-by-Step

Hillary Clinton said it takes a village to raise a child. It takes considerable planning, arranging, strategizing, and developing a plan to ascend into the upper echelon of corporate America. Every move that you make is as important as a grandmaster moving his pieces in chess. But it takes a coherent strategy to outdo your white counterparts and your ethnic competitors, and it won't occur by happenstance.

This chapter explains the building blocks that will set you up for success. It advises you to not limit yourself and see yourself only as a minority, shows you how to brand yourself, and emphasizes mastering interpersonal skills, which are as critical as technical skills. It also profiles a senior executive at AT&T to show how he moved up the corporate ladder by taking risks and being mobile. What you do in your early years can serve as the stepping-stone and launching pad for success. Finally, it also notes what traps and minefields to avoid.

Chapter 2: Choosing a Mentor

Handling the complexities of a major corporation when you're first starting out or even at a midcareer point is a daunting task. That's why finding a mentor or better yet multiple mentors is key to getting a positive start on building a corporate career.

At one major financial-services company, insiders call it finding a "godfather." You need a godfather to help navigate corporate politics, show you the ropes, offer challenges, and help promote you into new positions. That's where your skill and drive take over. But too many minorities play it safe and depend upon the company's mentoring program. Company mentoring programs are fine, but limited. You'll need to venture out and find your own mentors. We'll show you the keys to building your own network of internal and external mentors in order to set you up for future success. This chapter explains why finding multiple mentors may serve you best, how you can choose your mentor based on the company's culture, and the role of "situational" mentors. Moreover, we hear from an executive at Bear Stearns to learn how he found multiple mentors, and how one middle manager at Kellogg's hitched his star to a manager who became the company's first Latino CEO.

Chapter 3: Making the Right Connections—Network, Network, Network

Building a career involves developing numerous networks and tentacles in the outside world that will help you advance through the corporation; in many cases it may involve moving to another company.

But too many minority employees cling to their own ethnic group. Many African Americans do a superlative job of joining black networking groups, which is fine. The problem is that the circle becomes very limited, and the growth opportunities narrow and parochial. Since so few Hispanic, Asians, and African Americans have become CEOs and senior executives, your connections will take you only so far. This chapter will guide you to network outside of your own group, show you what works effectively, and train you to expand your social and professional network.

Tips in this chapter include developing a networking game plan, crafting your pitch, building an informal networking group of your own, and making the most out of conferences and events. You'll learn from two executives, one who started out at Avon and the other at Southern Bell, who used networking to advance their career. One even stated that "networking was essential to staying alive" in corporate life.

Chapter 4: Mastering Corporate Politics

Most minority professionals are disdainful of corporate politics, thinking that it will tarnish them. Since being tuned in to corporate politics is essential to success, it must be addressed in your early corporate years. You can't awaken in your eighth year on the job, after making many corporate miscues, and suddenly start to learn the skills. The earlier you master corporate political skills, the easier it will be to set the groundwork for advancement.

Here are the keys to playing politics without losing your soul. We'll speed things up by showing the skills you can master to use politics to your advantage and still maintain your integrity and peace of mind. For example, we discuss learning how to strategize, emphasizing making your boss look good, knowing who the decision makers are, getting the plum assignments, reaching out to all major players on promotion and leadership committees, and adapting your strategy to the corporate culture. You'll hear from several executives who learned to play corporate politics at JP Morgan Chase, Disney, and nonprofits as well.

Chapter 5: Strengthening Your Performance

Moving up the corporate ranks is not about your ethnicity or pigmentation; it's about performance. While it's difficult to quantify the effectiveness of a teacher or social worker, corporate professionals can be judged by their ability to help the bottom line.

Here are the tips to strengthen your performance and make sure your company has no choice but to promote you. Included in this chapter are learning to assess the corporate landscape, adjusting yourself to corporate goals, and focusing on bottom-line results. In this chapter, you'll read about a Bear Stearns executive who discusses how to align yourself with the company, a Sony human resources (HR) executive who learns how to adjust to bosses, and an IBM executive who manages more than four thousand people and advanced by taking on the assignments that others spurned.

Chapter 6: Turning Your Ethnicity
into a Competitive Edge

Too many African Americans, Latinos, and women end up swallowing their pride, suppressing their identities, and squelching their own uniqueness. It's my contention that being Hispanic, African American, or Asian, for example, is an asset. It brings a different perspective to corporate life and can help sell the company's product on a global basis. It can be turned into a competitive edge, not a disadvantage. But it takes strategizing and a certain mental outlook to use it as a strength.

In this chapter you'll read about four executives from the Uni-

World Group, Kang & Lee Advertising, the *New York Times,* and Disney Corporation who have tapped their ethnicity to advance. Relying on your knowledge of minority habits and cultures, learning how to specialize in researching minority psychology and market trends, yet expanding to the majority marketplaces are discussed in this chapter. Tips in this chapter demonstrate how to tap your ethnicity and use it to help the company, how to turn whatever doubts you have about your accent or background into a positive, and how to use this ethnicity to help your company go global.

Chapter 7: Making the Leap into the Corporate Suite

If you've challenged yourself, succeeded, and become a vice president or middle manager, you're now in the hot seat. The higher you go up the corporate ladder, the fewer the spots that remain, and the fiercer the competition. In this Darwinian universe, only the strong survive. But it takes considerable ingenuity to surmount the competition.

Furthermore, making it into the corporate suite isn't only about your résumé. Advancing isn't based on your title or job description, but on how you come across. It's the intangibles that count. Advancing up the corporate ranks involves having a presence, thinking on your feet, wowing people when you speak at a conference, and taking risks. Tips in this chapter include tapping into the CEO's vision and learning to win over people who are your subordinates while focusing on managing upward. Moreover, you'll hear from four senior executives from Scholastic Inc., Ford Motors, IAC/InterActive Corp, and Verizon on how they managed to enter the corporate executive suites. For them, it included living out their strategic career blueprint, constantly taking risks, being very mobile, and mastering intangible skills, mostly around personal relationships and communication.

Chapter 8: What HR Can Do to Level the Playing Field

Until this chapter, the entire book has focused on minority professionals taking control of their career, empowering themselves to succeed, and making all the right moves to advance. But admittedly, your company plays a major role in creating an atmosphere that will allow you to succeed and permit all employees to rise to their natural abilities. What exactly can the company do to create a level playing field? At many companies, the old boys' network prevails, and whom you know and whom you play golf with may take precedence over performance.

In this chapter, several experienced HR directors at A&P, Hitachi Data Systems, Exelon Corporation, and Wyeth Pharmaceuticals explain how each company has been developing its pipeline of minority talent, using an internship program like INROADS to introduce minorities, holding senior majority executives accountable for interviewing a wide range of candidates, and changing the culture to ensure that the company's senior executives reflect its diverse customer base.

An HR director at a major financial-services company in New York recently asked me, "Why are we constantly losing our talented African American and Hispanic staff?" Isn't it ironic that HR people desperately want to learn how to retain their talented minorities, when so many minorities hit the five- to seven-year glass ceiling and say good-bye to corporate life?

I call it a clash of cultures. Companies don't understand what makes minorities tick, and many minorities don't grasp the underlying realities of what it takes to succeed in corporate life. This conflict between the culture of corporate America and the culture of minorities needs to be bridged. This chapter sees the issue from both vantage points and explains exactly what it takes for companies to retain staff, and what it takes for minorities to reach out to HR departments in order to realize their potential.

Glossary

Here's the overview of what expressions like "branding yourself," "blockers and tacklers," "deselection," and "nesting" really mean.

INTRODUCTION: DEVELOPING A STRATEGIC CAREER ROAD MAP—CREATING YOUR OWN PERSONAL SUCCESS PLAN

YOU'RE BLACK, LATINO, female, or an immigrant, just graduated from a leading college and starting your career at Procter & Gamble, Accenture, Citigroup, Disney, or another major corporation. Raised in the barrio or on the other side of the tracks, you've worked hard, graduated college, overcome the jeers of your high school classmates who called you "brainiac," worn a new dark suit to your interviews, and used all of your charm, guile, and undergraduate education to get hired. And now you think the world is yours for the taking.

Not so fast. Most young, talented, minority professionals think the company is going to go out of its way to help them succeed. They read magazine articles and expect that working for one of the Top 50 Companies for Diversity will lead to senior executives inviting them to lunch and grooming them for big jobs. Having overcome so many obstacles just to enter the corporate world, they think society will respond to them *because* they're different.

But in most cases, corporations don't care if you were raised in downtown Chicago, hip Miami, ethnic Queens, or inner-city Detroit. Indeed, the corporation won't be looking out for you at all. Despite every major company's having a diversity program, the percentage of people of color who become middle managers is minuscule, and the percentage of multicultural candidates who become senior managers is well below that. In fact, the majority of blacks, Latinos, and ethnics who join corporate America leave after five to seven years. Corporate America loves to roll out statistics about the number of blacks, Latinos, and women hired, but it hides the fact that most depart faster than you can say "glass ceiling."

And hitting the glass ceiling and knocking your head against a granite wall are what most talented minority employees and females end up doing. Most ethnic employees that I've met as the CEO of one of the nation's prominent executive recruitment firms in the United States with a dedicated practice in diversity eventually say adios to corporate life, avoiding the corporate world of politics, mentoring, and networking. Some go into teaching, others pursue entrepreneurial opportunities, but most get chewed up faster than a Hershey's kiss.

Most corporations are doing a very effective job of diversifying the workplace. Twenty years ago, African Americans, Latinos, and immigrants were only a blip on most corporate organization charts, but now, due to diversity efforts, minorities constitute a sizable 35–40 percent at many companies. But one problem arises: though companies bring minorities into their respective organizations, most do a disastrous job of promoting them into mid to senior positions. Only six African Americans and one Latino are currently CEOs of Fortune 500 companies, and just a handful of women have advanced to CEO roles. Almost all CEOs are white men, and most board members, senior executives, and managers are also white. What happens to the talented minority professional?

Studies show the disparity between minority staff hired and promoted. A study by Donna Blancero and Robert DelCampo for *Hispanic MBA* magazine in 2003 showed that Latinos constitute over 10 percent of the entire workforce, yet only 1 percent of all executive officers and 1.7 percent of boards of directors are Hispanic. That means that Latinos are hired but fail to make it to the upper echelon in senior management, where they could set hiring practices and hire people who understand the Hispanic culture. The same is true for African Americans, Asians, and other minorities.

But it doesn't have to be this way. Minority members don't have to face a dead-end crisis, a paralyzed career, a forced exit out of corporations due to frustration and stagnation. Provided with a career road map, skills, and an inside look at how corporate executives operate, minorities can use this essential advice to start planning their advance through the corporation the minute they are hired.

My introduction lays the groundwork by setting out the six steps that it will take to succeed and surmount the obstacles: (1) creating a strategic blueprint early in your career, (2) building a career step-by-step, (3) choosing a mentor, (4) developing one's own network, (5) mastering corporate politics, and (6) turning your ethnicity into a strength. I'll also add a final chapter aimed at human resources to help them find ways to court and retain talented minorities and stop the exodus. Each chapter advances your knowledge, offers action tips, and shows you the way to surmount the obstacles.

I admit that the forces that inhibit people of color from rising in the corporation are powerful. But they can be overcome. It will entail taking one step at a time and advancing up the corporate ladder until you rise to the top. I'm asking you to be smarter, more strategic, and more nimble than your competitors who sit in the cubicles surrounding you.

Building a strategic road map for success involves "doing your homework," just as in high school and college. Except this time it doesn't involve writing essays or taking tests as much as conducting extensive background research on the companies that you go after to ensure that they embrace diversity and inclusion. It involves planning your next job while you master your current job. Developing a plan means establishing a network and learning to publicize your own accomplishments without turning into an egomaniac and alienating your colleagues. Executing these steps will enable you to create your own personal success plan and develop an approach to move up the corporate ladder.

Knowing the Unwritten Code

Corporations try to prevent you from unlocking their unwritten code. They don't want you to know that with few exceptions, people of color have been kept out of the power corridors of most corporations. And many CEOs view hiring minority managers the way many homeowners view a neighbor's selling a house to a person of color. A number of homeowners feel that if one African American or Hispanic moves into the area, many others will follow, and the neighborhood and property values will decline (a belief that is almost always proven false). "There goes the neighborhood" has turned into the unwritten code of "There goes the corporate suite." Many executives at the senior or C level (chief executive office, chief operating officer, chief financial officer, etc.), and their respective boards of directors, fear that if a person of color is named CEO, COO, or CFO, he or she will select other minorities as senior executives and they will seize control and deprive whites of the power base that they have solidified. Of course, these fears have always proven false, as exemplified by the staffs of

Richard Parsons, CEO of Time Warner; Carlos Gutierrez, former CEO of Kellogg's; and Ken Chenault, CEO of American Express, which are predominantly white.

In addition, many senior managers are threatened by the practice of hiring people of color to join them in the executive suites. Why does that outspoken, bright African American, Latino, Asian, or woman unnerve them? On one level, it's the fear of the unknown. Since many senior execs hail from Ivy League and other privileged colleges, where the 4 percent African Americans and 3 percent Latinos of the school tended to stay together, they've had little exposure to people of color. Many were reared in segregated communities and choose to live in suburban communities that lack diversity. Further, they are blind to the fact that hiring alternative voices that understand how to reach out to minority customers will increase the company's revenue and improve its return on investment. Bottom line, companies that can overcome their narrowness of thought can strengthen their balance sheet while improving the diversity of their senior management team.

Hence, minority candidates have to identify the few companies that are trailblazers, appreciate diversity of thought, and want to shake up and diversify their corporate offices. And that means keeping your antennae up at all times, reading the *Wall Street Journal, Fortune,* and *Forbes,* along with ethnic publications such as the *Network Journal* and *Diversity Inc.* For example, a 2004 article in *Diversity Inc.* ranked PepsiCo as the best workplace for African Americans and Latinos, and a 2004 *Wall Street Journal* article discussed Steve Reinemund, the CEO of PepsiCo, who devoted 1 percent of its revenue growth or $250 million to new products inspired by diversity efforts. Further, eight of his senior managers adopted an employee affiliate group (including African Americans, Latinos, Asians, and women), identified three talented people in their group, mentored them, and had to report to the CEO about their development.

Why the Top Fifty Diversity Companies Aren't Always Top

Despite PepsiCo's being named the number one workplace for minorities, and the other companies that make the top ten and top fifty lists, I recommend that you peel away the onion. Reporters who write these articles are not on the inside and often rely on data supplied by the company, making these ratings relative and impressionistic. Often these articles reflect more hype than substance. The best company may still need to go a long way to promote more minorities and build career paths for them. Don't rely exclusively on magazine articles; conduct your due diligence and go beyond that to ascertain which companies offer the best opportunities for minorities.

In addition, insiders will likely tell you that even progressive companies such as PepsiCo have their limitations. That's because "blockers and tacklers" operate in senior management positions; they give lip service to diversity, say all the right things, and then promote only their colleagues and friends who look and think like them, undermining the company's goals to expand into a wider array of executives. Hence, you need to perform due diligence on whether the finance, HR, operations, or marketing director is a true diversity proponent, or will block and thwart your development and career. Once you enter the company, I recommend that you seek out diversity champions who judge employees by performance and try to avoid the blockers and tacklers, who prefer rewarding and promoting like-minded and light-skinned colleagues.

That explains why, though most corporations proclaim that they operate on a "level playing field," it's usually tilted, and not in your favor. In order to level the playing field, minority candidates have to initiate, excel, and strategize so they can have a fighting chance to advance. Companies like to proclaim that quality performance is rewarded, not whom you know or which country clubs you frequent. But the reality is, whom you know matters greatly, and playing golf at the right suburban country club *does* matter. Nonetheless, I'll guide the high-achieving minority along so he or she can surmount that obstacle, too. Overcoming the unwritten rules in corporate America is key to success.

Mistake #1: Resting on Your Laurels

I've met a myriad of talented minorities who enter corporate life with the right credentials and polished communication skills, and think that all they have to do is show up to work and they will be recognized. The MBA from a leading university gets you into the corporate corridor, but now the hard work begins. Many people of color think showing up at the corporation will suffice, but outdoing their majority counterparts requires devising a strategy and career plan. And that involves performance, networking, being mentored, and learning what your company expects.

Mistake #2: Myopia

Many minority candidates get bogged down in their day-to-day corporate responsibilities and walk around their office wearing blinders. Instead of looking for opportunities, seeking the next job, pursuing challenges beyond their job description, and participating in professional conferences, they focus only on the minutiae of their current job. That behavior leads to spending many years in the same job, but getting typecast, and never moving on to the next rung. If you're in finance, find out what business areas are doing. Don't develop the back-office syndrome. Use your current knowledge to seek the next challenge, and take off the blinders.

Mistake #3: Getting Stuck in the Gender or Ethnic Trap

Many women in corporate life spend their time talking with other women, networking with other women, joining women's employee affinity groups, and rarely interacting with men. Similarly, African Americans join the African American network, Latinos the Hispanic network, and everyone stays in his or her own silo. And when people of color close off networking opportunities with white counterparts and downplay meeting with senior managers, who are mostly white men, it makes moving up the corporate ladder that much harder. Don't get stuck interacting with only your own ethnic group, because that cuts off too many growth and networking opportunities.

Mistake #4: Ignoring or Discounting Your Ethnicity

Hiding or downplaying one's ethnicity or gender is a trap that too many Latinos, Asians, African Americans, and even in some cases women fall into. Too often, they feel that if they shared their culture or ethnicity, they would be perceived as diluted talent or an affirmative-action hire. Learn to capitalize on your ethnic background, not ignore it. Use your ethnicity as a strength; seek out ways to maximize revenue because of your knowledge of what the African American, female, or Asian market offers. If you're working for Avon and sense that women are looking for a new kind of fragrance, share that info. Don't hide behind your gender or ethnicity (more about this in chapter 6).

Mistake #5: Shyness Is Not a Virtue

Asians, in particular, are known for not wanting to call attention to themselves, and many people of color share that attribute. It's okay for white men to toot their own horn, but ethnics often wait until someone takes notice of them. That's a way to cut off your own power. Learn to publicize your efforts, just as Sheila Lewis, a former Quaker Oats employee who is profiled in this chapter, did.

Build a Success Plan

Ethnic employees need to create a success plan for themselves in order to surpass their majority colleagues. Many of these colleagues, whose parents graduated from college, belong to the right fraternity, play golf at the right country club, and attend the right parties, enter the corporation with several advantages. What the talented Latino, African American, Asian, or female must do is catch up and seize the competitive edge. But creating a success plan is not like filling out tax forms that move sequentially. Each person has to create a customized strategic career blueprint based on his or her age, education (whether or not he or she has attained an MBA), and field.

Success plans are helpful guides but not panaceas. Your rise through the corporation depends on your performance and your ability to reach out beyond your business. The more networking you do and the more task forces you can join to meet other senior executives, the more you will boost your visibility in the company. Developing a success plan puts you on a path, but your performance carries you through.

You need to establish your own personalized game plan. If you've majored in finance, establish whether you want to work for a Big Four company or a corporation. Research whether the company fully believes in diversity and promotes high-performing minorities or only gives it lip service (more later about how to conduct that research). Do you want to be a trailblazer, establishing your own path to advance in the corporation because so few minorities have advanced, or do you want to work for a company that is already promoting minorities?

Establishing your own personal success plan entails creating a blueprint for where you'd like to be in the next five years and how you expect to get there. It's almost as if you're designing your own flow chart: here are the challenges that you want to take on in one box, here are the mentors that will help you along the way in another box, and here are the steps that have to be taken to get there. Most corporate workers are mired in the day-to-day and, because companies are changing so rapidly, spend their day "putting out fires." To differentiate yourself from the masses, and most of your colleagues who come in with certain advantages, you need to plan ahead.

Map Out the Next Five Years

Jot down on a piece of paper where you'd like to be in your career in five years, in ten years, in twenty years. What will be your next job? How will that job help you advance to future dreams? What challenges must you take to move up? What skills must you acquire to broaden your portfolio? What actions can you take in the next few years to make it happen? Be specific. Include the skills you must master to move up. Consider keeping a journal that tracks your progress. Jot down what "land mines" operate so you'll know what to avoid. Include your successes, such as joining a task force, and note which senior managers you've made contact with.

Research the Company

Researching the company is a prerequisite. What the company says about itself, such as "We treat minorities well," and how it really operates are often at odds. You need to research which companies are striving to create a level playing field, and which are not. In my executive recruiting experience, Pitney Bowes in Stamford, Connecticut, for instance, has an outstanding number of minorities in senior positions. Pitney Bowes walks the walk and doesn't merely indulge in fancy rhetoric or get listed as a top fifty diversity company, which is usually more about taking out full-page ads, particularly in ethnic trades, than really treating minority employees well. We'll show you a little later how to research which company is a good fit for you.

By conducting an Internet search of Boeing, for example, and contacting your alumni network, you can perform your own personal due diligence on the company.

- Will there be opportunity at Boeing?

- Are the barriers that held minorities back falling?

- Is the St. Louis aerospace and defense division open to people of color?

- Does its Chicago headquarters (where it recently moved from Seattle) encourage its minority candidates to advance?

- Is there room for opportunity in the higher ranks in a company that has had homogeneous upper-level managers in the past?

- Investigate its diversity site; review what achievements it touts.

- Show initiative; gather as much information as possible.

But if you're starting out, how can you learn the inner workings of the corporate culture? Tap your own network. For example, contact your alumni organization at whatever college you graduated from and ask it to recommend someone who works at your new company. Most alumni will immediately feel a kinship with you since you're both "brothers," "sisters," or alumni who have the same college connection. Ask the alumnus or alumna to meet you for lunch, coffee, or an after-work drink. Find out what the success criteria are. What is your division really looking for from a new employee? What opportunities are available to get ahead, get you noticed, and show your natural talents? What qualities and skills are bosses looking for? What can you do that goes beyond your normal job description? The more information you can elicit and the broader picture you have of the overall corporate culture and the specific culture within your department, the more poised you'll be to move up the ladder.

It's critical to understand the culture of the organization you're joining. The more information you can garner about what makes the United Way, the Federal Reserve, or Time Warner tick, what qualities senior managers are looking for in a talented executive, and which skills the organization respects, the more you can build a successful corporate career. Every corporate culture is different, and not every culture can be learned from reading the company's mom-and-apple-pie mission statement (respect others, listen to others, be a team player, and the like). In addition, you'll have to do your homework regarding the company's real attitude toward diversity or multicultural inclusiveness. Some companies embrace it, some encourage it, and some give it lip service while undermining it.

For example, if you were interviewing at Boeing Corporation and did your homework on the company, you would have learned that Boeing's diversity efforts were different from those of other companies. While many companies adopted diversity efforts as a business imperative based on highly competitive markets, Boeing, and one competitor, Airbus, dominated the aerospace and defense market. Faced with less domestic competition and few major global competitors, Boeing was slower to introduce diversity efforts. Hence, most of its senior managers were white men who came through the ranks and operated more in an old boys' network than at other companies, where that system was fading. As government regulations enforced equal-opportunity guidelines encouraging companies to interview a wider range of candidates, Boeing slowly entered the diversity landscape.

Target, which has been playing the number two role in the retail field to eight-hundred-pound gorilla Wal-Mart, has a different culture from Boeing's. The Minneapolis-based Target is known for its results-dominated, bottom-line culture. It has made strides in its diversity efforts and gone out of its way to hire midlevel managers of color. Target has also hired minorities for its board of directors, a positive sign. Yet the tendency to hire a homogeneous majority group has kept it from making great strides in hiring senior-level Latino, African American, and other minority candidates.

Were I being interviewed straight out of college by Target, I'd ask about the specific career opportunities that await me. Can I create my own success plan and find opportunities? Will I be able to be hired by profit-and-loss areas and not forced into ethnic marketing?

Is there mobility? Will I have opportunities outside of Minneapolis? Will I be able to choose a mentor? Are there employee affinity groups? Try to research the company's ethnic networking groups, and ask questions about opportunities for women, African Americans, Asian Americans, Latinos, etc.

Here are some questions to ask:

1. Does the company recruit at Historically Black Colleges and Universities (HBCUs) and Hispanic-Serving Institutions (HSIs), and if so, what is its track record for hiring alumni?

2. Has the company participated in INROADS, the nonprofit organization that promotes minority internships? If so, what percentage of INROADS alumni has it hired? How many alumni have been retained?

3. What type of involvement does the company have in the community, and does it offer community projects in lower-income communities? Donating money to diverse communities (not necessarily low-income areas) is often a great indicator of a corporate citizen that embraces inclusion at many levels, not just recruitment.

4. What is the company's mission statement, and does it include diversity/inclusion as part of its values?

5. Has the company been sued for employment discrimination? To research this, try a Google search like "Exxon discrimination" or "Exxon OFCCP" (Office of Federal Compliance Contract Programs) or "Exxon EEOC" (Equal Employment Opportunity Commission) to search for background.

6. If the company was sued, what were the terms of the settlement agreement, and has it been in compliance with the settlement decree?

7. Who are the people of color at the top? How did they attain their position, and how many years have they been in place? To research this information, try Hoover's (www.hoovers.com), a database that provides company profiles; Microquest, (www.microquest.com) and go to its "Shattering the Glass Ceiling" section, which includes diversity data on Fortune 500 companies; the *Network Journal* magazine (www.tnj.com), a magazine and Web site aimed at African American managers; and the Executive Leadership Council (www.elcinfo.com), an organization of more than three hundred African American senior managers. Also check out columns such as "People on the Move" in ethnic magazines such as *Hispanic, Hispanic Business,* and *Black Enterprise.*

Avoid the Senior Executive Minority Trap

Most minorities who advance up the ladder and become vice presidents and senior vice presidents are known to be generous with their time, often serve as mentors, and want to see other minorities advance. But not everybody fits this description. Be wary of the minority candidate who rises up the ladder and then ignores his fellow Hispanic, African American, or Asian colleagues. Often it stems from lack of confidence and not wanting to show favoritism, or being fearful that others will think it was only affirmative-action programs that got him to the top. Others don't want to be branded as opening

the managerial door to their brethren at the expense of Caucasian performers. You have to scope out which minority executives will groom
you and welcome you, and which will want nothing to do with you.

Do a Self-Diagnostic

Perform your own self-assessment. What strengths do you bring to
the company, and how can you use those strengths to advance your
career? What areas do you need to work on, and how can you develop
them? If you're a strong performer but hate making presentations,
take a course on speechmaking, join Toastmasters, or take one of the
American Management Association courses. If you come on too
strong, take an anger-management program. If you tend to be passive, consider assertiveness training. If you need more education, enroll in an MBA program.

I encourage people to ask questions. The more feedback you can
elicit from customers, managers, and peers, the more adjustments you
can make. Though conventional wisdom says you have to placate
your boss, asking questions is almost always seen as a positive, unless
you're asking tactless or obnoxious ones.

Majority corporate employees often come in with advantages.
Their parents or relatives worked at IBM, General Electric, or Morgan Stanley, know senior executives, take the train with senior managers, and have friends who are on the board of directors. Minority
candidates often don't have those connections. Even with an MBA
from Rutgers or Howard, you have to compensate for your lack of
corporate connections. One way may be to consider taking some sessions with a coach. Coaching associations such as the Coach Federation (www.coachfederation.org) and the Worldwide Association of
Coaches (www.wabccoaches.com) can help you identify a coach in

your area. Though the cost is not slight, four or five sessions may go a long way to setting up your future. The coach can customize his/her advice, guidance, and tips to your individual background and goals. In fact, coaches, if asked, can offer tips on helping you with your own networking skills and how to find the right mentor.

In addition, the coach can help you learn to read the corporate tea leaves by figuring out what makes each corporation tick and what behavior and outcomes will lead to advancing through the corporation. Some companies want their employees to be team players, others want self-initiators, and still others require customer-service specialists. Coaches can help you select mentors, internal and external, who can guide you through the difficult passageways of corporate politics. Hiring a coach is a way to regain the competitive edge, avoid corporate minefields, learn which traps to avoid, and focus on problem solving and building success from the outset.

Fees for professional coaches vary greatly. Some may charge $200 a consultation and agree to only one session, while others may sell you a limited package of three sessions. Try to gather recommendations and call several coaches to see if their price range is reasonable.

Either with the help of a coach or, if money is tight, on your own, create a five-year plan. Where do you want to be in the first year? If you're working for Quaker Oats in marketing, you want to help boost one of its products. You want visibility in making presentations. You may want to join some employee networking groups and find a mentor (more about that later too).

Planning your ascent through the corporation starts the minute you begin researching your prospective employer. Just as you had to research colleges in order to identify the school that was right for you, you'll need to do the same homework for finding the right company to work for and then establishing a career plan. Don't leave your career progress to luck or happenstance. As a talented African American, Latino, ethnic, or woman, you've got to make things happen, create the opportunity, and build your own stairway to success (though others will help you along the way), because the odds are the old boys' network won't be helping you climb the organization chart to the top.

Further, I recommend that from the day you land your job, you keep your eyes open for your next career move, inside or outside of the company. I don't mean immediately contact an executive recruiter, but listen to your colleagues, assess the marketplace, learn what comparable jobs pay, note which companies are growing and hiring, and constantly explore what opportunities are out there. It is pragmatic to be open-minded and explore career opportunities with another employer to ensure that your skill sets are valued and current in the marketplace.

Start creating a strategic blueprint for how you expect your career to grow. Assess the culture to determine if it's slow moving or fast, whether it's expanding or contracting. Further, your age, education level, and job will influence your plan. If you're twenty-four and have a bachelor's degree, and this is your first job, you may want to be more patient than if you're twenty-eight with an MBA from Columbia and have already spent four years at a Big Four accounting firm.

Master Core Competencies

Gaining the core competencies is critical to your future success. But most managerial candidates have mastered the skills, have the credentials and the pedigree. The difference between the people who rise through the corporation and those who don't is the intangibles. The candidate who understands the company culture, can present himself as energetic and dynamic, not just low-keyed and understated, and can offer a vision to help the company will advance. Learning to read between the lines and understanding what the company wants are the skills that propel the candidate to advancement. It's not all about "me" but what value you can add to the company. Focus on what value you can contribute to the organization.

Once in the company, however, avoid the trap of trying to change its culture. Just because you're street-smart and college educated and were raised in the inner city does not mean that the culture of Coca-Cola, Hewlett-Packard, or Johnson & Johnson is going to bend to your needs. You'll need to fit into the dominant culture at work. Understanding it, defining it, and learning how to navigate the culture will go a long way to helping you gain some semblance of control over it. Not only does each company have a distinctive culture, but within the organization, fiefdoms exist with their own unique culture. So the finance world led by the CFO will have one culture, human resources another, each business area another, and so on.

Corporations have been very open about hiring talented multicultural employees. The diversity is good for the company's culture, has a positive effect on a wide array of customers, and reflects well on a company with a global outlook. However, as staff advances through the corporation, and the number of senior positions narrows, diversity efforts fade. The world becomes more Darwinian as top-flight talent struggles for success, and a select number of senior management positions are often based on whom you know and whom you've impressed more than actual skills. Relationships often matter more than skills, no matter what the HR department and the vision statement suggest.

After the Skills Come the Relationships

If it's relationships that will ultimately get the talented African American and Latino to surge ahead, then building relationships is key. If you're following my advice, you've already identified a former alumnus in your company to help you develop your success path. The next step is to get involved in the company's mentoring program. Some companies, but far from all, have structured programs that assign a new employee to an experienced mentor. Unfortunately, companies often assume that the Latino will relate better to another Latino employee, a woman to a woman, an African American to an African American, an Asian American to an Asian American, etc. But if the new employee has an MBA and the experienced employee has a bachelor's degree, the new, bright, and better-credentialed Latino may easily threaten the more experienced Hispanic. Still, establish rapport and learn as much about the inner workings of the company, its culture, and the specific culture of your organization as you can. Your mentor may well know the land mines to avoid or some hidden insight into what will help you to succeed in the corporation.

Now you have two mentors, one from your alumni organization and another from the structured mentoring program. But don't stop there. Align yourself with various other organizations, such as the Society of Hispanic Engineers, the National Association of Black Accountants, Women in Technology, and whatever group can offer you someone in your field who can help you read the corporate tea leaves. A former employee of Microsoft, Goldman Sachs, or 3M may have a considerable amount of insight into the inner workings of the corporate culture. Learn about the corporate culture, ask about what works, and the more viewpoints that are offered, the more you can learn and make informed decisions about your career plan.

Identifying the right mentor (and we'll explore that in much greater detail in chapter 2) takes talent. When Luis Nunez, for example, was starting out in marketing at Kellogg's Mexico office, he started getting close to Carlos Gutierrez, who was managing director of Latin American sales. Gutierrez impressed him because of his "attitude of success," Nunez says. Gutierrez made everyone in his division at Kellogg's "feel as if you were doing the best job that you could do." From Gutierrez, Nunez learned the qualities that it takes to become a leader. "He was always motivating people to do better, looked people in the eye and listened," said Nunez. In 1998, Gutierrez was named CEO of Kellogg's, and in 2005 he moved on to become commerce secretary, and Nunez rose to become an international manager at Kellogg's, heading divisions in Colombia and South Africa.

When Sheila Lewis earned her MBA from Atlanta University in the mid-1980s, having earned her bachelor's degree from prestigious Washington University in St. Louis, she was bursting with enthusiasm and optimism about forging her corporate career. Bright, talented, articulate, she had all the characteristics usually associated with success. Upon earning her MBA, she had eleven job offers but opted to launch her career as an assistant brand manager with the Quaker Oats Company in Chicago, Illinois. "In my mind there shouldn't have been anything that could have precluded my successful climb up the corporate ladder," she said.

In her first year, Lewis did all the right things. In charge of test marketing for Quaker Oats Squares, she helped introduce the product, which was a success. She handled a range of tasks and within a year was promoted to associate brand manager for Aunt Jemima mixes, a brand that was sluggish and in need of an overhaul. Lewis and the marketing team helped update Aunt Jemima's image and repositioned the product. Beyond her marketing responsibilities, she was developing sales material and managing a $30 million budget and doing all the right things to advance her career.

Toot Your Own Horn

But in retrospect, Lewis recognized that she failed to make certain strategic moves that hampered her career. Despite the fact that she was an instrumental member of a team repositioning a once tired brand, she didn't manage to publicize her own efforts in the corporation. In addition, and perhaps most damaging, she was never able to secure a mentor. Later, she realized that the responsibility for tooting her own horn and securing a mentor rested with her. In her words, "Someone needs to know you in high places, someone needs to be prepared to stand up for you, someone in a position of high influence."

Because Lewis was driven, smart, and assertive, she presumed that senior executives at Quaker Oats would notice her. After only two years at Quaker Oats, Lewis moved on to become an assistant vice president at a subsidiary of First National Bank of Chicago; she ultimately spent a dozen years in corporate life at various companies but never got to the executive suite.

In 1997 she, like the vast majority of minorities who work in corporations, opted out of working for a large company and launched Flyin' West Strategic Marketing Resource Group, based in Fremont, California, a strategic planning and branding consulting company. Working on her own has brought Lewis the success that she was never able to achieve at Quaker Oats. Though Lewis took risks and changed jobs, she never achieved beyond a midlevel manager and never quite mastered the art of corporate politics or secured a mentor. But as a consultant, she garnered top clients through her own savvy and expertise.

What can we learn from Lewis's corporate experiences? Two key things: One, if you're starting out at a corporation, your personal characteristics and good work will advance you only so far. Good work won't be recognized unless you initiate, get yourself known, reach out to senior executives, and make that part of your own personal success plan. Two, you can't fully succeed on your own. You need to align yourself with mentors and supporters who will notice your efforts and help you advance your career.

Once you accomplish something, as Sheila Lewis did, find ways internally to let your supervisor and managers know, without coming across as boasting. Suggest that you present your marketing accomplishment at a staff meeting, or at an external organization meeting. Is there some news hook that could work into the company newsletter or the increasingly visible intranet sites?

Your strategic blueprint might look similar to Sheila Lewis's:

1. When you start your first job in marketing, finance, operations, or HR, ask yourself where you see yourself moving within two to three years. In most cases, it's advantageous to make a lateral move or a strategic move up the corporate ladder rather than staying pat for too many years.

2. If you're an assistant brand manager, as Sheila Lewis was, leverage your skills for your next move. How can you move from brand manager to new product development, which is exactly what Sheila did? You leverage your skills and

transfer them elsewhere. Think outside the box. Don't think that because you're in HR, you're stuck. The skills you master in HR will help you in sales, for example.

3. If you're an assistant vice president, think about what you have to do to advance to vice president. Lewis moved from First National Bank to the CoreStates Bank of Delaware and continued her climb up the corporate ladder.

4. If you find yourself peaking at vice president, use your mentoring network and professional contacts to ascertain what you have to do to move up one more step. Do you have to create a new project? Increase revenue? Boost sales?

5. Finally to enter senior management takes more than skills; it involves relationships. Whom do you have to meet and impress and network with to advance?

Lone Wolves Always Stand Alone

Bright Latinos, talented African Americans, enterprising women, savvy American Indians, and self-initiating Asians often stand out in high school and college. Trained to be independent and often leery of the majority, these talented ethnics operate as loners, making their way through college on grit, determination, and independence. But then the new employee starts working at Colgate-Palmolive, Wells Fargo, or Xerox, and everything is about the team. Becoming a team player is what most companies want, in addition to promoting independent, critical thinkers, but cooperating and listening to colleagues and being responsive to your teammates is also essential for corporate survival. Nor is this a contradiction, since team players must also look out for their own interests. If you've attended one of the Historically Black Colleges and Universities or Hispanic-Serving Institutions, you may have had less experience integrating with white people. Becoming part of the fabric of the team and learning that a true mosaic is what most corporations are seeking is critical to succeeding.

Furthermore, the talented minority professional can add value to the team. If you stay true to yourself, your culture, and your background but learn how to be a team player, you can add your different perspective, which can only enhance the team. As long as you're cooperating with everyone, not becoming aloof or withdrawn, you will add value to the team. Be passionate about what you do, but leave your ego at the door and recognize that prima donnas get left behind. Team players thrive in today's culture.

We'll talk more about networking in chapter 3, but it's critical that minorities reach out beyond their ethnic group. Don't just join a diversity group, where you'll be one of ten bright, talented people of color. Instead, if you're in the PR field, reach out to the Public Relations Society of America, a national organization of PR professionals, where you'll stand out as an outspoken minority member and make a name for yourself; or join the Society of Human Resources Management if you're in the HR field.

Toughen Up; Create Positive Energy

Just as in sports, where the mental outlook can make the difference between winning and losing, your approach toward the corporation can determine whether you're going to advance through the corporation or get stuck early on. Too many minorities create self-fulfilling prophecies by figuring they don't have the right pigmentation or accent to advance. Defeated before they start, they set low expectations and regrettably attain them. "Shoot for the stars," Ralph Waldo Emerson once advised his readers, and that's as true today as it was in the mid-nineteenth century.

Avoid the "Woe Is Me" Syndrome

Too many minority candidates fall victim to the "woe is me" approach. Stop considering yourself a victim or outsider and get rid of the oppression mentality. Growing up as a minority, you think that white people are always out to get you, slight, belittle, or exploit you. Certainly that might have happened to you, but most whites aren't out to attack or exploit you, or anyone else.

A friend of mine who shopped at an upscale department store used to think that the sophisticated sales staff paid her no mind because she was black until a white friend of hers complained about how the store's arrogant salesclerks ignored her. Salespeople there slighted everyone, but the African American made it a racial issue. Many African Americans, Latinos, and ethnics expect to be slighted, and often get that result, or perceive that they do. Leave the oppression viewpoint back in your old neighborhood. Come to the corporation with an open mind, a positive outlook, a willingness to succeed, and a clear plan for success.

While most minorities often belittle companies' diversity programs, and do so for good reason, what's ironic is how minority employees deliberately separate themselves from the company's mainstream. Have lunch in many corporate cafeterias, and it will often look much like the high school lunchroom, where African

Americans dine with African Americans, Latinos with Latinos, and Asians with Asians. Minority employees need to look at issues from a dual perspective: your own outlook and the majority's viewpoint, balancing the two. If you view everything from a black or Latino perspective, it's myopic and ultimately cuts you off from seeing things from the company's viewpoint, and advancing.

Planning your ascent through the corporation also depends on maintaining a positive attitude. Many of your colleagues will yield to cynicism. "Jerry got promoted because he played politics, knows the boss, plays golf with him at the country club, went to the same college, but we'll never get ahead. We're black/Hispanic/a female/an immigrant, speak with an accent," colleagues will say. Cynicism will get you nowhere. Those who are cynical become complacent or morose, or indulge in backstabbing, all of which are one-way tickets to corporate stagnation. The minorities who advance have the drive, personality, and energy to distinguish themselves. Impervious to their negative colleagues, they rise above their fellow employees and are distinguished by their ability to make a difference, add value to the company, and go beyond their job description. Maintain a high morale, and people will take notice of you. Succumb to low morale, and you'll never advance.

Action Steps

If you're following my advice, here's what you should have accomplished by reading chapter 1 on establishing a strategic success plan and implementing our suggestions. Here are the steps that I recommend that will help you develop your strategic success plan, differentiate you from your colleagues, and help start your ascent up the corporation. Check off what you've accomplished and note what still needs to be done in order to start your advance up the corporation.

- Write a preliminary plan of where you'd like to be in the next five years and what specific steps it will take to get there.

- Research the company that you are considering joining or have started in. What prospects are there to advance?

- Begin to tap your networks to establish contacts at your company. Since so much of moving up depends on forming relationships, the faster you can start meeting people higher up in the corporation, the better your chances of advancing will be.

- Identify your strengths and weaknesses. Develop a career blueprint for overcoming your limitations.

- Consider hiring a coach who can help you develop your five-year strategic plan and develop a concrete approach to working on your limitations.

- Focus on your core competencies. In order to move up, performance is a prerequisite. You must master the basics and then refine and polish everything else.

- Begin to form relationships in the company and outside your department. Reach out beyond your ethnic group. If you're Hispanic or African American, make sure to look for role models and senior executives who are white who can take you under your wings.

- Start taking credit for your contributions. Many minority candidates don't want to bring attention to themselves.

The people who advance learn to publicize their own efforts without antagonizing fellow team members.

- Create positive energy. Avoid falling victim to the "woe is me" syndrome.

- Now you're ready to start strategizing, as they call it at many corporations, or planning your career step-by-step (which moves right into chapter 1).

- Start your own journal. Chart where you want to be, what kind of progress you're making, and what you have to do to advance.

BUILDING YOUR CAREER STEP-BY-STEP

■

S UCCESS DOESN'T HAPPEN overnight except in sentimental
Broadway musicals like *42nd Street,* where the understudy re-
places the star and instantly becomes famous. In corporate life, planning your ascension through the organization requires the skills of
a chess grandmaster. In this chapter, I lay out how you can make a
name for yourself, build your corporate reputation, and stand out
from the crowd in order to surpass the many colleagues who also
want those high-powered managing-director and senior executive
slots. In short, I map out how you could build your career from day
one of being hired to enable you to surmount the obstacles to advance
in the corporation.

The Broadway musical *Seesaw* featured the song "It's Not Where
You Start, It's Where You Finish." Where you start can influence (but
not determine) how far you rise up the corporate ranks. Too often I
see minority candidates being lured into and agreeing to launch their
corporate careers in roles such as ethnic marketing, public finance, or
government or community affairs, rather than assuming a line and

operations role that has direct impact on the company's bottom line. "You're African American and we'd like you to start selling Crest to the African American market, or doing community affairs in inner Detroit," the HR rep will say. "You can help recruit people of your own ethnic background" will be another ploy that will play on your civic virtue and conscience. In this chapter I'll propose ways to avoid being pigeonholed as an ethnic marketer, which can lead you into being trapped.

Once you secure your first job, start investigating how to move up to the next rung, internally within your organization or outside with another company. Your supervisor/manager will likely serve as your initial ally in your pursuit. Without being overly aggressive, obnoxious, or self-serving, start asking questions about how he or she moved up, the skills required for the job, who are the key contacts that you need to develop, and what his or her director/manager looks for in staff that wants to move into the fast lane. Consider also meeting with your supervisor's boss to discuss similar topics, as long as your direct manager won't see this move as circumventing him or her.

One way to get ahead in most companies is to turn everyone into your ally. The administrative assistant to the senior manager of your department may be low on the totem pole, but she or he may be a hidden treasure trove of knowledge. Nearly every piece of information goes through him or her, so establishing a strong rapport can help you to learn what's going on before everyone else does. Remember, you're becoming a strategist and intelligence gatherer. Everyone in the department—colleagues, your immediate supervisor, the senior manager, and administrative assistants—is a potential ally of yours.

Your attitude and performance will determine whether you have what it takes to climb up the corporate ladder. For example, *Crain's*

New York Business published an article in early 2005 about the difficulty faced by many African American men in business because they often don't smile, look gravely serious and sullen, and come across as defensive. In the ghetto, this defensive posture made good sense because there were so many threats to their safety or manhood. But in the corporate world, their sullen stare alienates people and often forces too many of their colleagues to keep their distance. Overcoming this defensive gesture by opening up and changing their facial expression is necessary to advancing their career.

Possessing the right attitude and being a self-starter, an open, performance-driven team player, sets the tone. And then the emphasis must be on making the right moves.

Hence, I recommend becoming proactive about moving up the minute you land your first job. That doesn't mean avoiding mastering your job at hand. Clearly becoming a top performer in your current role is a prerequisite to success. But too many minorities think that by sending their résumé to Monster.com or an ethnic job board once a year, they're taking an aggressive approach to job hunting. They're not. Most top performers, in fact, avoid the massive Internet job sites, which are equivalent to cattle calls, because they attract thousands of résumés, so one high-performing individual like yourself, can't stand out from the masses.

Mistake #1: Resisting Assimilation

Too many minority rising stars "silo" themselves off from their colleagues. Mistrustful of others, not knowing who is racist and who gives diversity lip service, many people of color detach themselves from the corporate mainstream. That error can be fatal when it comes to gaining trust, becoming noticed, and securing first-rate, challenging assignments and reaching out and expanding your network. To succeed in corporate life beyond being a solid performer, you need to become the quintessential team player, collaborative, outgoing, and reaching out to colleagues and forming relationships throughout the organization. You become the go-to person at conferences, help recent graduates make the transition into corporate life, and turn yourself into the all-around network/team player. At all costs, avoid becoming isolated and cut off.

Mistake #2: Getting Pigeonholed

Some minority professionals are proud that they have created a place for themselves in the corporation. They're the good guy or woman who is a junior-level marketing person who does a decent job, gets 2 percent raises, and watches colleagues advance up the corporate ladder. Though they are as bright and effective as their colleagues, they are complacent and just plain satisfied to have a job. The minority performer who succeeds is the one with fire in the belly. Strive to reach your maximum potential. Being talented and capable isn't enough unless you learn to play corporate politics, network, master relationships skills, and instill some positive ambition in yourself that ultimately is evident when people work with you. Don't settle for complacency; maximize your chances of reaching your full potential.

Mistake #3: Playing It Safe

I see many talented corporate minority workers who are risk averse. It's as if the dominant culture has brainwashed them to play it safe or not think enough of themselves to stretch their own talents. The senior managers who move up take risks. See the section on Carlos Linares, "How One Executive Built His Career," in this chapter. He could have stayed in human resources and languished, but he took the risk, moved his family, entered a profit-and-loss area, and because he did well, catapulted his career.

Mistake #4: Passive Go-Getters Won't Succeed

Besides getting trapped in dead-end jobs, too many minority candidates are laid-back, passive, wait for an opportunity to come to them, as if they wanted to be anointed for the many talents they possess. The passive worker or job seeker is an oxymoron that describes people who get stuck in quicksand and watch their career aspirations wither away. Instead of being laid-back, the ambitious minority who is poised for success has to become opportunistic, proactive, and assertive. "The meek shall inherit the earth" worked fine for shepherds during biblical times, but it won't be as effective in twenty-first-century corporate America.

Mistake #5: Being Turned into a Token Minority

Falling into the trap of being the token Latino, Asian, or African American is an easy hole to fall into. Avoid it. You're not the Hispanic guy in finance, or the Asian guy in HR. You are a three-dimensional specialist who can comment on how majority people react to marketing campaigns, not just comment on one ethnic group that you're closely aligned with. Similarly, don't limit yourself because you see few minorities in higher places. Taboos are meant to be broken, and if you outperform and outmaneuver your competitors, it's you who will be calling the shots.

If you're not a member of an exclusive Harvard, Yale, or Cornell club, where senior executives socialize and network with one another, then you have to take alternative approaches to getting known, reaching out, and marketing yourself. That means thinking about meeting senior executives at cocktail parties, attending the lectures that most of your colleagues shun, participating in conferences that may not be as scintillating as an episode of *CSI* or *Desperate Housewives.*

When you do meet someone, strategize to maximize your opportunities. In addition to hobnobbing at conference, lectures, workshops, and employee affinity groups, I tell candidates, opt for meeting in informal settings. If a senior executive meets you and invites you to be interviewed in his office, suggest meeting at a local diner instead, where it's less likely that calls or drop-ins from colleagues will interrupt the meeting. One, you won't jeopardize your current position by being noticed by an ex-colleague at your competitor's office, and also you'll put your best foot forward and be more relaxed in the informal setting.

Don't Limit Yourself by Viewing Yourself as a Minority

In planning your career for the long haul and anticipating becoming a middle manager and senior executive, it's critical not to limit your options or opportunities. Too many minorities view themselves as an outsider, or see themselves as the token African American, Asian, woman, or Hispanic in the organization and never expect to move up. Seeing yourself as a high performer who adds value will help you to build a career and not limit yourself.

Though proud of his Mexican heritage, Luis Nunez, who spent over twenty years at Kellogg's in marketing and other areas and is currently a principal in Brandslab, a Weston, Florida–based consulting firm specializing in boosting Latin American sales, admits, "I didn't spend my time thinking of myself as Hispanic. Don't focus on being different. Work hard and help the company meet its goals." His focus was on performance. Everything was performance driven, and he moved up the corporate ranks based on his performance, his helping Kellogg's meet and exceed its revenue goals. His being Latino was instrumental because he understood the Latin American market, and yet at the same time it was immaterial to his success. Nunez was able to maintain his own culture and show pride in it, but when it came to succeeding on the job, it came down to performance, not his ethnic background.

Strive to Fit into the Mainstream, Yet Maintain Your Ethnicity

But gradually, after being a corporate executive for nearly two decades, Nunez became acculturated to the majority culture. He began to play golf and loves playing it. He joined a country club, where many senior executives play golf on weekends. He would drink Budweiser after playing a round of golf, and there would be little difference between being a polished Hispanic senior executive and a majority senior executive. He has adapted to mainstream corporate values while still retaining his Mexican heritage.

Avoid Getting Pigeonholed

There's nothing wrong with starting in ethnic marketing, public finance, public affairs, HR, or community affairs. Certain self-initiating corporate workers can begin there, get to know people in various businesses, and then transfer out of those specialties into line and operations roles or profit-making areas. But too many minority candidates start their career in these fields and get stuck there and sink as if in quicksand. Receiving minor raises every year, they toil in these "safe" areas, never coming close to getting involved in impacting the bottom line. If you want to build a success plan and rise up the corporate ranks, it's showing you can turn a profit or increase revenue in your business that makes the difference. Ethnic marketing and public relations, though valuable areas, have their limitations. The more you can get involved in sales, operations, and frontline businesses, the better you can prove that you're a valuable asset to the company.

Again, some minority candidates have advanced from ethnic marketing and PR jobs, but they are few. There are two major problems with these jobs. First, most people in the organization don't respect them, see them as "soft" and less pressured because they don't have clear profit-and-loss responsibilities. Second, because there's no P&L associated with them, success in performance is very subjective. On the other hand, a sales manager who beats his revenue goals by 20 percent is a rising star. Whether he's African American, Latino, or Asian, that 20 percent sales boost speaks volume in the company.

Turn Your Supervisor into Your Ally

Another key to planning your career is working with your direct supervisor. Explain to your supervisor/manager that you want to build a career and immediately want to become part of the business side, or agree to spend two years in ethnic marketing with the provision that you can transfer over to mainstream marketing. Too often supervisors, afraid to come on too strong in performance evaluations, write bland comments in your performance appraisal. That leads to your getting stuck. You need to be challenged, and you need to take risks. Make sure your performance appraisals include stretch goals that can help you advance and move you into profit-and-loss areas.

Become Just Like Coca-Cola and Disney, Known for Something

In order to be noticed and stand out from your peers and plan your ascent early in your career, you have to differentiate yourself on the job. But unlike painters, who possess their own unique style, how does a corporate employee distinguish herself? By branding herself.

Branding themselves is one key skill that minority professionals can use to help them overcome their lack of connections and build their career and establish their reputation. Branding involves differentiating yourself from your competition and becoming known for one outstanding trait. Just as Coca-Cola quenches one's thirst, Disney means family entertainment, and Donald Trump symbolizes a can-do mogul, anyone at a company can brand himself. Administrative assistants who specialize in creating unique PowerPoint presentations can brand themselves and become invaluable to the company, just as audit or financial managers who specialize in handling the Big Four consultants can brand themselves, too.

Brand yourself by deciding what your main skill is and then develop it. Then let the organization know you possess that skill by publicizing your efforts. Are you the wittiest copywriter at your ad agency, the financial adviser who appeals to affluent minorities, or the IT consultant known for her high-tech skills? Any of those skills can be branded to differentiate yourself from your colleagues and help build your career step-by-step.

But becoming known for one skill is not the only way to brand yourself. You might even tap your own ethnicity to establish a brand. Maybe your company is overlooking the Latino market or doesn't know how to reach it, or doesn't know how to attract affluent African American women. If you can start a venture that appeals to them, you can help your company's bottom line and build a brand for yourself.

Branding yourself takes ingenuity and creativity. You may have devised the most innovative way to sell your packaged good, originated a special way to market your product to the multicultural community, developed an original made-for-television film that no one at your company has thought of. And then it requires spreading the word that you originated the idea.

Another way to brand yourself entails launching a volunteer organization, which can help strengthen the company's reputation and improve its standing in the community. Meet with your manager and explain what you're interested in doing and get his or her buy-in. Since most companies publish several internal newsletters, contact them to write a story about the new grant, nonprofit organization, or employee-networking group. Toys for Tots, the Make-A-

Wish Foundation, AIDS walks, tutoring groups, and working with local artistic groups are all endeavors that can motivate you and help brand you within the company.

How One Executive Built His Career

Carlos Linares started at AT&T as an account executive in the mid-1980s and spent time working in HR in Latin America, but realized that if he didn't extricate himself from HR, he'd be stymied in his career. He told a mentor that he wanted to return to sales. Why leave the security of HR for the risky area of sales? the mentor responded. "I'd have more responsibility, and I'd be able to make decisions," said Linares, who left Lucent Technologies (which was a subsidiary of AT&T) in the mid-1990s, and resides in Davie, Florida. Making that decision to go into sales propelled his career.

"That career move helped me to shine. Latin America was a wide-open market, and people who were qualified had room to excel," Linares notes. Furthermore, sales opportunities often create level playing fields because profit-and-loss statements create clear-cut winners. Linares helped grow Lucent's business in Latin America from $185 million to $1 billion from 1997 through 1999. In the process, he advanced to senior manager. "Promotion was based on performance. I moved up because of my work ethic, results, and the fact that I could lead people and work effectively in the corporation across several organizations," he says. He left Lucent in 2002 during a severe downsizing when the first of the dot-com high-tech bubbles burst.

Another factor in Linares's rise in the corporation was his ability to find and gain the trust of a mentor. Art Medieros, a senior manager at Lucent, mentored Linares and "taught me a lot about being an executive and running a large, complex operation." Medieros also promoted Linares twice and, upon Medieros's retirement, recommended Linares for regional president, which helped secure his promotion.

Linares was also mobile, moving his family from Miami to Mexico. "I wanted the opportunity to live in Latin America and expose my children to another culture. I liked the idea of their speaking English and Spanish," he says. Had Linares not been mobile and had he decided to live only on the East Coast, he would likely not have advanced up the corporation.

In a competitive corporate environment, only the strong survive and thrive. No matter how intelligent you are, whether or not your MBA is from Wharton or Harvard, your independence and political know-how will differentiate you from your colleagues. Moreover, while many white employees were reared in an environment where their father or uncle was a corporate employee and they've learned through osmosis how to survive, many minorities hail from working-class backgrounds. Corporate life is as foreign to many minorities as living on Bora-Bora or the Fiji Islands. Hence, initiating all the time is required because you can't fall back on previous connections or the inner workings of the corporation.

Part of planning your career step-by-step involves emphasizing taking the initiative. You can't wait for someone to brand you, notice you, and recognize your accomplishments; you must proactively get your name out there, originate breakthrough ideas.

Publicize Your Efforts

No matter how handsome or attractive you are and how many A's you received in schools, most corporate executives will pay you no mind unless you earn their attention and respect. Part of planning your career and plotting your next move involves making sure influential people in the corporation know about your accomplishments.

If you're in marketing at a financial-services company, your role in a mergers-and-acquisitions deal must be spectacular in order for you to get noticed. Once you've been a member of an award-winning team, you must publicize your efforts. Send a note to the head of a burgeoning industry or association conference and ask if you can lead or join a panel. Get yourself noticed and known. Become your own publicist. There's nothing wrong with being modest and self-effacing, but in a Darwinian environment, it takes self-promotion to shine.

Become a Risk Taker

Too many minorities avoid taking risks. Focused on security and pressured by their family to play it safe, they don't want to leave the comfortable confines of their current job. But often the result of that false feeling of security is being trapped in one job, never being challenged, and never putting themselves in a position to advance. Just as Carlos Linares ignited his career by transferring into sales and moving to Latin America, you need to take risks and get out of your comfort zone. In addition, as we've said before, getting involved in profit-and-loss areas and helping the company increase revenue can be a prime way to advance. Spending your career in ethnic marketing can be stultifying and paralyze a career.

Looking at today's marketplace, the people who succeed are risk takers. Playing it safe and staying at your job for an extended period often leads to inertia, dashed dreams, and limited success. Landing that first job is a stepping-stone to creating a career path up the corporation. It takes planning, strategizing, ingenuity, and risk taking to advance. But the alternative is spending too many years in the same job, spinning your wheels like a car on ice.

Planning your ascent through the corporation is like a publisher launching a magazine. The launch requires forethought, a marketing plan and future planning to plot where the magazine will be in its first year and its fifth year, and a strategy to differentiate it from its many competitors. Risk takers must plan their corporate career the same way. The first job gets your foot in the door, helps build your credentials and résumé, and propels you up the corporation or into your next job.

Mobility May Be Necessary

In my experience as an executive recruiter, I've found that many minority workers like to stay put. If they're based in New York, Los Angeles, Chicago, or San Antonio, they often prefer living in cosmopolitan, diverse communities, where they can dine on southern food, rice and beans, or Philippine specialties, and not be isolated. Yet increasingly, planning a career and rising up the corporation involves being mobile.

When Sheila Lewis felt stymied at Quaker Oats, her first job out of college, she didn't wallow in pity. Seizing control, she took a risk and found a job in new product development at a First National Bank of Chicago subsidiary. "I knew I was in the middle of the pack; I wasn't a superstar," she admits. Her second job expanded her skills beyond packaged goods into banking. She could use her MBA in marketing and finance and yet go beyond it. That job led to being hired at the CoreStates Bank of Delaware and ultimately ascension to vice president at Visa USA/International.

Risk taking can involve changing both locales and jobs and, as Lewis exemplified, working in new industries. Starting in packaged goods, she moved to financial services, but later took a job as director of marketing at Lane Bryant, the clothing company. Too many minority employees get stuck in "silo" thinking and don't consider opportunities in other industries. If you've performed exceptionally in marketing at a pharmaceutical company, for example, those skills can transfer over to most industries. But again you're walking a fine line because moving too often marks you as not loyal to your company or raises questions about why you must move every year or two; so any move must be made strategically and judiciously.

I recently completed a search for a senior executive for sales and marketing at Cox Communications in Tyler, Texas. The executive who was chosen was African American, and recognized that the job was a springboard. It offered only similar pay to his previous job, but gave him an opportunity to broaden his portfolio of skill sets and responsibilities. He relocated with his family. If he needs to drive twenty-two miles to find an appealing church or ethnic eatery for dinner, he'll make the extra effort.

The More Entrepreneurial You Become, the More You Build Your Career Path

If the company you're working for has a track record of promoting minorities, you're on the fast track, and staying there can be the right move. Still, you need to consider changing jobs within the company to expand your skills, go beyond community relations, manage people, and take leadership positions. Carlos Gutierrez, who until December 2004 was CEO at Kellogg's before being named commerce secretary, started at the cereal company in 1975 and advanced for nearly thirty years. In the mid-1980s, he was named director of a Mexican subsidiary at Kellogg's, which caused his career to sky-rocket. "If you could design the perfect career path, it would likely include running your own line of business. That's where you get noticed and where you can put up good numbers and show leadership," he said. But Gutierrez took his risks within Kellogg's and never had to change companies.

Taking risks requires performing due diligence. Make sure that the new company you're considering is open to minorities advancing, offers networking groups, and has a track record for promoting diverse candidates. Only move if the job offers potential challenges. In today's marketplace, the spoils go to the employees who are relentless, passionate, and tenacious. And that invariably entails taking risks.

No matter what the mission statement of the company says, and even if the company was voted one of the top fifty places for minorities to work, you're going to have to overachieve to succeed. If the majority employee is networking at country clubs, you're going to have to spend more time at work, make more connections, launch more projects, network more effectively, and impress your bosses to keep pace. Don't ever sit back. No matter how glowing your performance appraisal, strive to take on more projects. If you're in finance, ask to work within the treasury function. If you're in communications, request a new challenge in the investor-relations field.

Ultimately, your performance will determine how far you advance in the corporation. By analogy, it's very much like baseball. The .300 hitters are the leaders who make the most money, and the .189 hitters get sent back to the minors to refine their skills. Whether you're Asian, Latino, or black is less consequential than how you perform. Colin Powell didn't rise to become general in the

U.S. Army because he was Jamaican or considered black; he advanced because of his performance, competencies, and ability to lead.

Build Your Personal-Relationships and Interviewing Skills

Many ethnic employees focus on building their core technical skills and overlook one necessary ingredient: their personal-relationships skills. If you were to study most successful senior managers, CEOs, CFOs, and COOs, many have the technical skills and also have mastered the art of personal relationships. They know how to interact with people, build relationships, and go with the flow. Consider the ex-military person who had the skills, know-how, and credentials, but failed to get the job because of a lack of interpersonal skills; personal relationships can ultimately make the difference between success and failure.

Mastering social skills also involves learning how to interview effectively. I've observed a multitude of minority candidates who have shot themselves in the foot when interviewed. For example, a Big Four accounting firm interviewed one financial middle manager, an African American woman with top-flight credentials. When they asked her about salary, the proper response would have been to not answer the question directly but discuss how she wanted challenges in her career and to help the firm achieve its goals. Instead, she explained that she was making $99,000 augmented by a $25,000 bonus and that if that bonus wasn't matched, she wouldn't make the move. The senior executives thought she had answered in an arrogant way and was more concerned with her income than with helping the company. She didn't get the job, undermined herself by not reading cues during the interview.

We recently submitted a candidate to become CEO of a new Hispanic bank in New York. He had worked for Citigroup and Marine Midland, possessed an MBA, and had solid credentials with strong and diverse financial and managerial skills. But the company wanted a dynamic leader, not just a competent person. During the interview, the chairman of the board was relaxed, informal, and engaging, wearing a sports shirt and Docker pants, casual attire for an executive conducting a formal job assessment. Yet our Hispanic candidate remained stiff and distant. And that wasn't the type of CEO that this bank was seeking. Our candidate, despite his MBA and credentials, failed to read the cues during the interview, and didn't get the job. Stubborn and inflexible, he was unable to adjust to a different type of chairman. Mastering social skills is as critical as gaining the right competencies.

In fact, executive recruiters refer to this phenomenon as "deselection," which is a euphemism for ruling out and excluding people who likely won't fit into the company's dominant culture. That can sometimes mean that minority candidates who aren't polished enough won't be hired. In order to build your career, mastering technical skills won't be suffice. It's the people skills that will separate you from the herd and help to ensure your climb up the corporation.

The Hidden Ingredient

If you're building your career step-by-step, you need to have all the essentials mastered. Another skill that few discuss and that is often ignored, but is critical to advancing, is listening.

In a recent book based on interviews with 188 CEOs of leading American companies and nonprofits, listening to others was one of the primary skills that many CEOs said was essential to their success. Listening enables people to discover the cues that will lead to success at the company. But too many corporate workers shut down listening and think that they have all the right answers. Listening to senior executives, HR staff, and middle managers helps you to learn what the company is looking for. And at most companies, what they're seeking is constantly changing as they acquire other companies, consolidate, and shift to a new marketplace. If you learn to stop talking, stop thinking of what you want to say, and instead listen to others and remember what they say, it will help you become successful.

Ironically, even when you're being interviewed for a new job or new position, listening is essential to success. The candidates who spend their time boasting about themselves but never ask a question about the company, its culture, and what kind of person the company is seeking may fall by the wayside.

Most people have a hard time listening, because they are impatient. Ready to chime in with what they want to say and impress their boss or colleague, they lose interest in and track of what someone else is saying. Listening to your co-workers and bosses provides new information and perspective on the company, and enables you to get to know others better. In addition, listening to your customers clues you in on their needs and helps you to anticipate what they will want in the future.

Learn to Get the Real Deal About
Performance Appraisals

In order to build your career, you need feedback. Just as golf and tennis enthusiasts take lessons from a pro who can offer feedback on their swing or serve, getting feedback from supervisors, colleagues, and customers can help strengthen your skills. Unfortunately, because of many companies' fear of lawsuits, minority members often fail to elicit honest feedback.

Human resources professionals will tell you that performance appraisals can be a tool to strengthen your career, discover your weaknesses, and learn how to improve in order to advance through the corporation. That may or may not be true for most majority employees, but in many cases, performance appraisals offer minimal benefit for minorities. Many managers and senior executives are reluctant to give honest feedback to minorities, fearing it will trigger an Equal Employment Opportunity Commission (EEOC) lawsuit and a backlash against them for criticizing minorities; and perhaps some don't want to help minorities advance. Put all of these factors together, and most minority performance appraisals obscure rather than reveal the real performance.

For example, Sheila Lewis says that when she received her performance appraisal at several companies, she got stock answers rather than personalized and individualized feedback that would help her advance. Feedback wasn't analytical or constructive.

An absence of feedback or support is much worse than critical feedback, which can be addressed. Often minority members get positive feedback, such as "You're doing a great job," which is also general and watered down, and not very helpful, either.

For these reasons, forming your own internal network, tapping your mentors, and establishing strong rapport with many people in the organization can prove fruitful. If your manager or supervisor won't offer honest feedback, find someone else in the organization, another senior manager whom you work with, who can offer honest feedback. The more honest the better because then you'll know more about whether you're about to be derailed or are on the fast track, whether you're thought of highly but have to make improvement, or whether you should update your résumé and consider a move to another business or company. Uncovering where you're excelling and where you need improvement can help you strengthen your competencies.

Take the initiative with performance appraisals. After you've worked on a project and contributed a better-than-expected effort, ask the supervisor or manager for a letter of commendation. Start building your own performance feedback.

Conquer the Intangibles; Advancing Is About More Than Skills

No matter if you obtain honest feedback, master core competencies, and listen to others, you're still going to have to do more to outmaneuver everyone else who wants to move up the ranks. Mastering basic skills won't be sufficient to ensure becoming a senior manager or major player at a company. You need to master the intangibles to build a career.

Besides learning how to deal effectively with others and play politics effectively (described in chapter 4), minority candidates, like majority candidates, will be judged by their performance. The best way to advance in the company is to maintain positive relationships with everyone and outperform everyone at the same time. What are the success criteria for advancing? Clearly you need to possess all the core competencies and skills, but that's a starting point. Often, it's the intangibles that make a difference: how you read people, ability to motivate others, sense of humor, skill at not taking everything personally, facility to reach out to people of different cultures and backgrounds, and tactfulness so as not to offend people. We've all met doctors who know their medical terminology but have no sense of their patients and lack an effective bedside manner. I like to call it the "likability factor."

Part of that likability involves being a team player. The more collaborative you can be, the more effective you will be for the organization. The day of the lone wolf has passed, since most corporations operate in teams and revere an ability to cross-sell the company's products.

When we identify talented minorities for senior positions, most everyone interviewed possesses the right technical skills. For a CFO job, the candidate will have mastered the financial basics and has the requisite the on-the-job experience. What enables one candidate to get the job while the others falter is almost invariably chemistry. Most senior managers and HR executives hire someone that they can easily get along with, play ideas off of, someone who listens to other people and has the right blend of substance and sociability. I can't tell you how many times we've presented a highly qualified professional for the job who didn't get it because he hyped himself up, didn't read the other people in the room, didn't ask the interviewer questions, and spent the entire interview rambling on about himself. Focus on the intangibles as well as acquiring the proper skills.

Master Dealing with Your Peers As Well As with Superiors

Managing upward plays a crucial role in planning a career. But so does learning to manage your colleagues, who can make or break your career. Maintaining positive relationships, becoming a team player, going out of your way for others, and impressing everyone on your team, not just your manager, are all skills that must be mastered. But oftentimes when the minority employee gets recognized, is deemed an all-star, or is promoted, envy in white counterparts is triggered. Learning how to handle your colleagues is another skill that must be mastered in planning your ascent.

Rightly or wrongly, when a high-performing minority candidate rises in the corporation, it often triggers a strong reaction of resentment from his or her majority peers. Suddenly, the affable co-workers who always asked how your weekend was and filled you in on what was going on turn stone cold, frigid, and frosty. They refuse to acknowledge you, or bite their lips and talk with you only reluctantly. Some majority candidates feel threatened; others feel that you have taken their promotion from them. Others will accuse you of benefiting from favoritism, or attribute your rise to affirmative action, when in almost all cases, it's meritocracy at work.

What you need to do first and foremost is not take any change in someone's reactions personally. You haven't done anything wrong, and there's no reason to feel guilty. Not everyone is going to love and cherish you forever. But try to turn the negative into a positive. Involve such a person in a project—make him part of your team or task force. Provide a challenge for him. Reaffirm what a good job he's doing. Stay positive all the time, without being patronizing. Win your formerly friendly peers over and prove that you're the best for the job without showing any resentment toward any of them.

Take a Yearly Assessment

If you're just launching your career, you'll need to take your own annual assessment of whether you're making progress and meeting the goals of your strategic blueprint for success. How will you know if you're making progress? There are several ways. You'll know whether you've developed positive rapport with your bosses and colleagues or not. Are you included in meetings? Is your opinion sought? Are you given challenging assignments? If you answer yes to most of these questions, you're making significant progress. If not, you may be facing "tissue rejection," a term used to describe organizations that say they are ready for diversity but, like an organ that is rejected in a transplant surgery, aren't actually ready to embrace it. You'll also be receiving 360-degree performance feedback, which should provide insight into your strengths, limitations, and progress.

If you sense that you're not making strides in your career and that your strategic blueprint isn't resulting in career progress, then you have to calibrate your next career move. Planning a career is like playing chess against a grandmaster. Every move must be plotted, and every future move triggers another response in the future. If you're feeling stymied and ignored, then you need to consider your next move. One issue to be considered also has to involve how your boss's bosses view diversity. Is your boss a champion or ambassador of diversity who views all candidates on a level playing field and values diversity? Or is he/she just giving lip service to it but prefers majority candidates who play golf at the local country club? If your boss isn't a proponent of diversity, then study the company and find a leader who is, then consider an internal transfer. What you shouldn't do, however, is stay stuck in your job for five to ten years, fearing to make a move, or just getting out of Dodge after five years because your majority counterparts are being promoted and you're not. Don't lapse into the "woe is me" victim mentality or syndrome. When in doubt, get yourself activated and refer to your strategic blueprint.

The trick is planning your next move. Too much job-hopping and you're viewed as suspect, someone who only cares about herself and not the team. Staying in place at a dead-end job that isn't challenging, though, does not help you or the company. You may want to seek the counsel of a headhunter or search consultant, or check with your mentor, who can help orchestrate your next move; or you may know a former colleague who is looking for someone talented like you.

Please note that there's one aspect of planning your next move that hasn't been mentioned: money. In my view, money is a secondary factor. For example, if you're working at Kellogg's in a dead-end job for $52,000 but are offered a challenging job at Clorox for $5,000 less that helps you to strategically introduce a new product, grab it. In five years, you'll be earning $30,000 more than you would be if you had stayed put at Kellogg's. Again, planning your next move is like playing a grandmaster in chess, so every move counts.

If your career has stalled, jump-start it. Sometimes you don't even have to change jobs. If you're working in audit or accounting, take on a new IT project. Challenge yourself. Create some new opportunities. You can create your own visibility by launching a volunteer project, developing a new video for the department, or creating a conference to get your department known. Sometimes self-initiating is the best way to tackle low recognition, rather than waiting for someone else to tap you on the shoulder or pat you on the back.

Also analyze whether your multicultural insights and additions are valued or disregarded. If you're working for a fragrance company that refuses to market to the ethnic community, and management doesn't want to hear your suggestions, that says volumes. If you're working for a pharmaceutical company that doesn't promote its drugs in minority neighborhoods and won't listen to your suggestions, that says volumes. If your fresh, innovative thinking is being ignored, then it's time to look for another challenge.

However, if you see majority counterparts, who you think don't match your skills, moving up the corporation, it's time to evaluate what's going wrong. Are you being turned into the token ethnic in the company? Is your boss not a diversity champion? Is moving up based on whom you know and whom you socialize with, rather than job performance? If the culture of your business isn't open to minority candidates, then it may be time to find a new company that is.

Be Bold and Audacious

Kindness and humility are fine traits, but not the hallmark of most senior managers. Assertiveness and risk taking are qualities that lead to rising in the corporation, particularly for minorities, who often lack the social connections.

If the playing field were actually level, talented minorities wouldn't have to be bold. All they would have to do is perform well, exceed their peers, and let their true talents shine. But the reality is that many minorities are held back because their accent is different, they don't belong to the right country club or live in the right suburban neighborhood, or they haven't been designated by a senior exec as the chosen one. Hence, they have to work harder and be persistent and relentless in their pursuit of senior roles within the corporation.

Though companies will never admit it, minority candidates have to overcome hurdles and doubts that majority candidates do not face. I've found that interviewers at major corporations often have lingering doubts about minority candidates. Did this person achieve his position through affirmative action? Diversity programs? Quotas? Or did he achieve his success based on his own merits?

For example, a bright African American senior IT executive recently interviewed for a high-level job at a major cable company. He wowed the management team of interviewers, but was never hired. Because he didn't know anyone personally at the company and because that company was going through some major transitions, one of his meetings was curtailed into a twenty-minute quickie interview. Unnerved by the brevity of the interview, and spending his time responding to a limited number of questions, he never got a chance to ask questions himself. The company rejected him, partially because he didn't ask any questions or show initiative. He didn't take the rejection passively. Instead, he pleaded his case to HR and was subsequently asked to return for another opportunity to present his strengths to the organization. This kind of relentless persistence and bold action is what it often takes for talented minorities to succeed.

Action Steps

If you're following our advice, you won't be stuck in putting out fires day to day, but will start looking into the future to plan your career. That first job is just a stepping-stone to launch you into your second job, prepare you for your third job, and catapult you to promotions and your move up the corporate rungs. Check off what you've accomplished so far and note what you have to work on to advance.

- Having secured your first job, start thinking about the next job that will boost your career. Write down the steps you need to take and the skills required to be considered for this job. Make note of who at your company can help you make the necessary introductions to HR people and senior managers in that area. Set up a meeting with them.

- Instead of sticking with the people in your limited business, start expanding your network. The more people you can meet in other areas, the more opportunities can arise to avoid being pigeonholed and to move out of your current area.

- Brand yourself as the best operations guy, the marketing whiz, or the HR specialist who devises innovative solutions.

- Start publicizing your efforts, without coming across as being arrogant. Look at your internal newsletters and see what types of articles are written. Suggest ideas for your area. Reach out to professional organizations; volunteer to speak at conferences and join committees. Start getting your name out and about and beyond your narrow work area.

- Become a risk taker. Playing it safe is fine if you're a postal clerk, but won't lead to advancement in corporations.

- Like Carlos Linares, start thinking about changing locales. To move up in corporate life, you may have to change jobs, and where you're living, several times. But if your company offers plenty of challenges internally, look to move within.

- Think like an entrepreneur. What can you do to generate more revenue for your company? What new markets can be tapped?

- Turn everyone you interact with into your ally: your boss's administrative assistant, your direct supervisor, and your colleagues.

- Don't limit yourself by thinking of yourself as the female marketing expert or the Latino operations guy. The more expansively you view yourself, the more expansively others will see you.

- Plan your career like a chess grandmaster. Every move you make should result in advancing your career. Jot down your next move, and the move that you figure would be most beneficial after that. Plan ahead; strategize; develop your own success plan.

2

CHOOSING A MENTOR

■

FOR MANY MINORITY candidates, getting in the door at a Pitney Bowes, IBM, or United Way is such an accomplishment that
they think they have it made. But getting in the door is like a baseball pitcher who gets the other team out in the first inning and thinks
he has a win. The game has just begun.

Every step you take in your corporate life entails chipping away at
the granite wall. Directly above you, the company has placed a low-
rising ceiling that's hanging over your head. The company wants you
to do well, but as you rise up the ladder and close in on this ceiling,
the buzzards are circling. These buzzards want the promotion and expect that they'll get it because they were born with a sense of entitlement, and have the connections and breeding that you may lack. But
the point of this book is that if you play your cards more effectively
than they play theirs, you can surmount the obstacles. Obtaining the
right mentor who can be your number one supporter and help you
navigate up the corporate ladder may be the speediest way to make
your move.

Every day, you'll need to chip away at this glass ceiling. And that requires total focus, superior performance, staying on top of everything, securing mentors, improving your network (see chapter 3), staying on top of your strategic blueprint, and outthinking, outmaneuvering, and outperforming your peers. Finding the right mentor who can make all of your moves easier will lighten your load as you climb toward the apex.

This chapter walks you through specifics of how to choose a mentor, what a mentor can and can't help you with, and what you must do for your mentor in return.

Mistake #1: The "I'll Do It on My Own" Syndrome

I vividly remember one candidate, a bright African American who had everything going for her. She graduated from one of the Historically Black Colleges, moved from a packaged-goods company to the telecommunications industry, wore blue-tailored suits, and always looked the quintessential professional. She garnered superior performance appraisals and was highly respected at her company; at times, however, she displayed arrogance. When I first met her, I asked her if she had identified any mentors. She pooh-poohed the idea, saying she didn't need one. She said she had the right qualifications, the right MBA, and was street-smart and astute about the corporate world.

But she wasn't astute about needing a mentor. She eventually rose to become a midlevel manager at a financial-services firm, switched jobs several times, and then burned out and left corporate life to become a small-business owner. When I asked her what mistakes she had made in her corporate career that prevented her from rising further, she acknowledged that not pursuing a mentor led to her downfall. Rising in the corporation by your own devices is difficult, if not impossible; a mentor or series of mentors can show you how to better navigate up the corporate ladder.

Everyone in a corporation needs a mentor, a godfather, or a rabbi. It doesn't matter what you call the person, but it's almost impossible to advance through the corporation on your own, like a marathon runner, racing in front of the pack. For example, as talented as Ken Chenault is, it is unlikely that he would be CEO of American Express if it hadn't been for Harvey Golub, the former CEO of AmEx. Getting promoted, winning challenging positions, becoming a vice president, and climbing the organization's narrowing pyramid are based on your performance and gaining the confidence of senior managers. If you try to do everything on your own and are stubborn enough to think that you can succeed as a solo act, you will wind up bailing out of the corporation faster than you can say "exit interview." Having overcome the rough-and-tumble streets of Oakland, Baltimore, or Richmond, the striving minority thinks that the only way to make it in the corporation is to depend on thyself. Trust thyself and rewards will come.

But those minority candidates are, in most cases, deluded, and many find that without identifying a mentor, they become thwarted in their ambition and ready to jump ship in that critical five- to seven-year juncture. Swallow your pride and recognize you must find a suitable mentor or, better yet, multiple mentors to help you navigate the corporation. Your mentor's or mentors' feedback and advice on your strategic career plan are critical to your success.

Mistake #2: Choosing the Wrong Mentor

Do not choose a mentor who isn't savvy about corporate politics, along with being well connected, nurturing, and equipped to guide your ascent in the corporation. Choosing a mentor who is a "nice guy" or "decent woman" may not be enough to get you where you want to be. Further, selecting a mentor who is isolated or outside of the corporate mainstream may also be of limited value. Instead, choose a mentor who is well respected and embodies the dominant values of the company. If you're at Coca-Cola, which has seen its profits plummet, you need to find an innovative, strategic thinker who can help boost the company's revenue and help teach you to think outside the box. Status quo won't work there anymore. Hence, you have to select the mentor with the right characteristics who is primed to ascend the corporation and help you make the right strategic moves.

Mistake #3: Choosing Only a Mentor Who Looks and Thinks Like You

Many people choose a mentor based on who fits most easily into their comfort level. If you're a Latino guy from Los Angeles, you look for another Hispanic guy from California who shares your values. Or an African American woman seeks someone who looks, acts, and thinks like her. It makes the mentor-mentee situation that much easier, because there's no cultural divide to overcome. For many people, that's the easiest option and can be very effective. But also consider choosing a mentor who can do the most for you, rather than one who won't challenge you or will blindly support you. In fact, for many aspiring minorities, choosing the majority mentor who is higher up in the corporate chain can be a catalyst to success. That's why corporations refer to mentors as "godfathers" or "rabbis," because they will help you handle corporate politics in ways that like-minded mentors may not furnish. If you're participating in the company's formal mentoring program, you're more likely to be paired with a majority person.

Mistake #4: Stopping at Only One Mentor

If you're lucky enough to be selected for the company's mentoring program, you may think you have it made. You've been placed on the fast track, have access to a mentor who can groom you, and now you can sit back and rest on your laurels. But one mentor isn't necessarily enough, and other mentors can come from outside your company. Your uncle who spent five years at Apple Computer, your neighbor who is a corporate training consultant, your minister who may offer spiritual advice to help you overcome your anxiety, and your college fraternity president who now heads HR at a leading pharmaceutical company may all be candidates for mentoring you. While one mentor may help you with corporate politics, another assists with making connections, and another recommends what cutting-edge books to read. You gain from each of them.

Mistake #5: Getting Stuck with the Wrong Mentor

Because you've been assigned a mentor in a corporate program doesn't mean that you have to stick with him in perpetuity. If you sense early on that the relationship between you and your mentor isn't clicking, ask the program manager if you can choose another mentor. Consult with your mentor and tactfully explain that you want to obtain a different viewpoint; don't offer too much criticism that will come back to haunt you. Some mentors may be threatened by you, even if you are less experienced in the company. If you have an MBA from a leading college and your mentor doesn't, he may see you as a threat to replace him. Why mentor and groom the person who will lead you into early retirement? Don't get stuck with a mentor who is not much help or, worse yet, may stab you in the back. If the mentor relationship isn't working, find another who will, but exit gracefully without burning any bridges or offending your mentor.

Choosing the Right Mentor

If you think you can conquer the corporation and progress on your own without the assistance of a mentor, the odds are strong you'll be leaving the corporation out of frustration after a certain amount of years. Moving up is so complex and depends so much on the support of others that it's very difficult to advance as a solo act. Further, the minority professional who thinks she can advance by her own merits often has the character to venture off as an entrepreneur, rather than operate as a corporate team player. Mentors are as necessary in corporate life as parents are to their offspring, only the relationship is adult to adult.

In creating a positive mentoring relationship, performance plays the major role. Mentors will respond to you only if you are a high performer *who can cast a positive image on them and help their career.* Stated most bluntly, no one wants to be associated with a poor performer who is late to work, doesn't fulfill his duties, and is eliciting subpar performance reviews. Humans act primarily out of self-interest, so the mentor must be energized by working with you, enjoy your company, willingly give up time to meet monthly for lunch, and feel that you are destined to move up. If you move up, that sheds positive light on your mentor and his or her ability to groom talent.

Overcoming the Unwritten Rules

But for many minority employees, mentoring seems like a secret code among their majority counterparts. Majority employees will speak about how their mentors recommended that they take a certain training program or apply for a certain job, while the minorities feel left out in the cold or isolated in Siberia. It becomes very evident to minority professionals that mentors create a mutually beneficial relationship. Don't feel left out in the cold and allow your Caucasian counterparts to seize opportunities while you look on from the sidelines. Get into the fray. Seize the initiative to identify your own mentor(s), whether in a formal program or informally.

During the interview process, some companies tout their formal mentoring program, describe its successes, and promote the fact that 30 percent of their minorities participate in it. But despite the growing emphasis on diversity and inclusion, only a limited number of companies have formal mentoring programs. Furthermore, most corporations won't tell you that, for the most part, you're on your own when it comes to mentoring. Even the companies that offer a structured mentoring program use it in a limited fashion to designate a fast track. And while minorities may constitute one-third of the program, that leaves many people of color outside of the loop. Even if you participate in the formal mentoring program—and by all means, if you're asked, you should get involved—one mentor won't suffice to surmount all of the obstacles. The more enterprising you can become when it comes to mentoring, the more you will set yourself up for success.

Some minority employees are wary of the formal program, thinking that they'll be paired with someone who speaks a different cultural language or will judge them as inadequate. Don't be scared off. You can make this mentoring program work for you, and you can develop a strong relationship with your mentor or ask to find another mentor.

The Onus Is on You

Whether you join the company's formal mentoring program or establish your own mentoring relationship informally, you are responsible for keeping the momentum going. It may be referred to as mentoring, but it's the mentee who fuels the engine and sustains the relationship. You can turn this into a high-octane relationship by pumping it up, meeting monthly, asking your mentor to lunch; or you can turn it into a quarterly get-together. The more you are invested in the relationship, the more dividends the mentoring relationship will pay.

Tips on Finding a Mentor

Raised in a religious environment, reared to be self-effacing and shy, some minority candidates are not naturally assertive when it comes to pursuing senior managers as mentors. One method that works very effectively is using third-party endorsements. If you have a friend from your alumni association, family member, or work colleague who knows a senior executive in your company, ask him or her to suggest that the senior manager serve as your mentor. In my experience, 75 percent of the people who are asked to serve as mentors agree to do it and react enthusiastically. For most managers, it's a form of recognition and an ego boost to share their expertise and nurture another person. If the potential mentor declines because of overlapping assignments, find another, but don't be discouraged.

Situational Mentors

You also don't have to choose one mentor as your be-all and end-all. Mentors can be selected on a project basis. For example, if you have questions about your compensation or your performance evaluation, you may choose a mentor who is knowledgeable in those areas. If a reengineering project is taking place, and you've not worked on one before, you can select someone with that experience. You can make it clear that you'd like limited advice on a given project and then you'll move on.

Choosing the Right Mentor Based on the Company's Culture

The best mentors vary, depending on each company's culture. Since most company cultures stress collaboration and team building, you should pursue someone who embodies these characteristics, rather than an autocratic manager who wields power in a top-down management style. The more nurturing the person, the better the mentor. I recommend seeking mentors who are well connected, who reach out beyond their narrow business area, and who are favored by the CEO, CFO, COO, or HR director. Associate yourself with a rising star, and the odds are stronger that you can accompany the fast-tracker up the management track.

In addition, find a mentor who has strengths that you lack. If your mentor is an expert in networking who relishes talking at conferences and doing interviews for the company, and you're shy or stubborn, choose that mentor. As previously stated, mentors who are threatened by bright people of color with MBAs or strong credentials can easily be skipped over.

Just as I urged you to conduct due diligence on the company you were seeking to work at, some research of mentors can be helpful. If you're participating in the formal or informal programs, find out whom your prospective mentor has assisted. Call these mentees and ask how accessible the mentor was, how supportive and helpful he or she was, and what the previous mentee thought of the experience. It can help you to avoid a bad fit and to find the best possible mentor.

Some companies employ group mentoring, where you have one mentor, but the mentor will meet with three or four mentees at a session. Those programs can be very beneficial because you learn from your peers as well as your mentor.

Link the Mentor to Your Strategic Career Blueprint

In the introduction, I discussed creating that strategic blueprint, which will lay out your future goals and how you expect to get there. Your mentor will help you along the way. At the risk of sounding like a character from *Dick Tracy,* the mentor supplies the "decoder ring" and helps you to understand the subtext and underlying tensions of what goes on in the corporation. That mentor operates as your navigation guide, fixing your course, modifying your direction, providing feedback on how you're doing. If you need to toot your horn, your mentor will let you know that. Your mentor should serve as a catalyst in moving you up the corporate ladder. The mentor will provide you with the guidance and intelligence to help you advance, so you won't need to take four years to move up or accept the next challenge.

Choosing a Mentor Outside Your Comfort Zone

Many minority employees naturally gravitate to a senior executive who looks like them, especially if the relationship is developing informally and not within the company's organized mentoring program. Women flock to women, African Americans to African Americans, and Hispanics to Hispanics. In many cases, they speak the same language, share the same cultural language, and have a more natural communication. If a mentoring relationship naturally evolves with someone of your ethnic group or gender, that's fine. Take advantage of it, but don't limit yourself to like-minded mentors.

Some minority corporate employees are reluctant to get involved with mentors who may be perceived as privileged, favored, or from the other side of the tracks. Don't be put off by this cultural divide. You can surmount this chasm between you and your majority mentor, even if the mentor grew up fortunate in Grosse Point, Beverly Hills, or Greenwich, and you hail from a working-class neighborhood or the ghetto. Take your cultural divide and turn it into a positive. You can supply your mentor with knowledge of global markets: what young people want, what the iPod generation seeks, what Latinos, African Americans, or Asians expect from your company. If you're sitting in the cafeteria with your friends, invite your mentor to join you, which will likely be perceived positively as a very inclusive gesture. You'll learn from your mentor, and your mentor will learn from you.

Benefits of Being Mentored by Someone
of Your Own Ethnic Group

Some minorities say it's easier to identify someone of your own ethnic group to serve as mentor. Kevin A. Stephens, forty-four years old and until recently a vice president of sales and marketing at Cox Communications, and who previously was a vice president at the Xerox Corporation, owes much of his rise to finding two African American mentors. As an African American himself, he found a "natural comfort zone" with a mentor who shares a similar background and understands what it is to be a minority in a mostly white environment. African American managers "see a little part of you in themselves," he says, and make an extra effort to mentor.

In his experience, a white senior manager would be a more difficult fit as an informal mentor. Majority senior managers have been surrounded by whites, often live in segregated suburban communities, golf at mostly white country clubs, and attend parties with peers who resemble them. "If you have a five handicap, your children attend the same school, and your wife works at a similar-type nonprofit, a minority member might hit it off with a majority manager. But the odds are you don't go to the same barbershop or church, and that relationship will be difficult," says Stephens, who was raised in Detroit but attended a multicultural parochial high school.

Ironically, Stephens contends that it's easier for an African American senior manager to mentor a majority person than it would be the other way around. Stephens contends that most African Americans who are moving up the corporate ranks know how to assimilate; otherwise they wouldn't be capable of advancing. As he moved up, he mentored some majority employees with whom he developed a positive relationship and who wanted to learn the ins and outs of marketing from him.

While Stephens was at Xerox and working out of Los Angeles, Barry Lathan, a vice president, took a liking to him and served as his first mentor. "He gave me counsel on what my next move should be. He helped me to become a sales manager. 'You take care of your performance, and we can talk strategy,' " Stephens says Lathan told him. Stephens recognized that superior performance was his responsibility, and Lathan recommended the right challenges for Stephens, which helped him advance.

In fact, Lathan helped him with actual deals. "We talked out negotiations. At times, he would sit in on negotiations, and having a senior-level manager helped cement deals," Stephens said.

Beyond deal making, Lathan introduced him to several senior managers. He introduced Stephens to a senior Xerox executive at headquarters in Rochester, New York, which helped Stephens land a new job and subsequent promotion at headquarters. "He also taught me that if I wanted to move up, I had to be mobile," Stephens adds, a theme often invoked by minority professionals interviewed for this book.

From his second mentor, Emerson Fullwood, the president of a division at Xerox, Stephens learned about the art of preparation. "He taught me to always be prepared, whether it was a presentation, report, or sales meeting. He played a key role in helping me get to the VP level."

Previously, I advised you to reach out and find majority mentors who have the right connections and can help you strategize. Minority professionals can benefit from establishing mentoring relationships with white senior managers, but Stephens proves that if mentoring relationships evolve from managers of the same ethnic background or race, that can be effective, too.

Overcoming Ethnic Inhibitions

In my recruiting experience, I've found that Latinos are often hesitant about participating in mentoring programs and identifying informal mentors. It's almost as if they want to be anointed by someone as being an effective worker, rather than going after the prize. It's like a woman who waits at home for a boyfriend to knock on her door, rather than participating in social events. In fact, many Hispanics can learn from many African Americans, who have become more assertive by finding mentors and being seen. If you sit back and are passive about mentoring, you'll find yourself without a mentor and stuck in the corporation. Lying back is fine for beaches, but not effective in corporations.

Cuban Americans, however, like Carlos Gutierrez, the former CEO of Kellogg's, have proven to be more assertive, and feel more assimilated than other Hispanic Americans. I would urge other Latinos to learn from the Cuban Americans, who have become more assertive in finding mentors, which helps them move up the corporate ladder.

The African Americans who have become CEOs at Fortune 500 companies, such as Ken Chenault at American Express or Stan O'Neal at Merrill Lynch, demonstrate how mentoring can be one strategy to help advance through the corporation. Chenault was mentored by Harvey Golub at American Express, a tough-minded leader who provided the challenges and connections that led to his ascent, and O'Neal was groomed by David Komansky, the former CEO of Merrill Lynch, a strategic thinker who was impressed by O'Neal's Harvard MBA and superior results.

Furthermore, study the majority men who feel a sense of entitlement. How did they identify a mentor? What can you learn from them? What does it take to become more assertive?

What Your Mentor Can and Can't Do

Mentors can provide feedback, guidance, a sympathetic ear, introductions to senior managers, networking opportunities, an experienced view of what it takes to succeed at the company. But no matter who your mentor is, your mentor can't replace or furnish you with the most necessary ingredient: performance. Some people think that once they've selected a senior manager as a mentor all they have to do is sit back and be taken along for a ride. It doesn't work that way. Your mentor will guide you, but your performance will carry you through. Keep your performance up and use the mentor as a source of feedback. If you don't have support from a mentor, you'll be the first one to go if there's downsizing, says one corporate insider.

Finding Multiple Mentors

Carlos Valle, the forty-six-year-old manager of Institutional Middle Market Sales at Merrill Lynch in New York, oversees a staff of seventy people in nine offices. He's considered a rising star at the company. Born in Cuba, he graduated from the University of Pennsylvania and has an MBA from the University of Virginia. When asked what the keys were to his ascent up the corporation so quickly, he replies that having "multiple mentors" played a significant role.

In his first job, at Aetna Insurance as a credit analyst in bond investment, Helen Young, an investment officer in the bond division, a totally separate business from Valle's, took him under her wing.

Young and Valle were not part of a formal mentoring program, but the two just connected as people. In fact, Valle has had a series of mentors in his corporate career, and in all cases the relationships evolved naturally and were never part of a formal program.

Young assumed a nurturing role for Valle. She offered practical advice about advancing at Aetna, but also cautioned him to be patient and not to expect to move up overnight. She stressed that his performance was the number one factor that would enable him to rise up the corporation. But Young also took practical steps to ensure that Valle met the right people. Though he was a junior-level employee at Aetna, she invited him and his wife to several social events at her house in the Hartford area. These social introductions helped Valle make connections that would lead to his rise up the company. When Valle would see one of the managers in the corporate cafeteria that he had met at the dinner party, he could more easily start a conversation or follow up on something that had been discussed socially. "When a job opened up within the division, these contacts enabled me to be considered for the position," he acknowledges. Young also contacted Valle to check up on his progress to ensure that his career was proceeding on target. "She took ownership for me and made sure I was on the right track," Valle admits.

When Seth Waugh joined Merrill Lynch's Corporate Trading Department in investment banking in 1998 (he is now a senior executive at Deutsche Bank), Valle was assigned to work with him. Waugh identified Valle as someone on the fast track and again, without ever joining a formal program, started to mentor him. In his first performance appraisal, Waugh said something to Valle that left an indelible impression. "You're very bright and capable," Waugh said to him. But he added, "When you walk into a trading room with a thousand people, you need to develop a strong persona so you stand out from the crowd and everyone notices you." People, he went on to say, need to recognize your expertise. Offer your assistance to people who are working on a deal, which will strengthen your reputation in Corporate Trading. "I found his comments to be liberating and encouraging and felt emboldened by them," Valle says.

In fact, Waugh encouraged Valle to "lead with performance," but added that "you have to make sure that people notice what you're doing." Waugh also reminded him to make sure that the company's senior executives and upper management, and his peers, were aware of his efforts. "He showed me that if you're good at what you do and know what you're talking about, you should project that," Valle reveals.

Not only did Waugh empower Valle, but he also promoted him. When Waugh left the corporate bond business and moved to asset-backed syndication, he told Valle that the right spot for him in the organization hadn't materialized. A year later, Waugh called him and offered him a position to replace a manager who had left for a position in Asia. Though Valle hadn't been a manager, Waugh believed in him, took a risk with him, and laid the groundwork for his success. Valle has been advancing since then, due to Waugh's mentoring.

Part of Carlos Valle's success at identifying mentors was his openness to people. People respond warmly to other people who are energetic, welcoming, and enthusiastic. Valle says, "I've always felt embraced by people in the corporation. I've always felt that other people treated me like a team member. I never felt limited in any way." The best mentor relationships, he says, "happen naturally. When there's enough personal connection, the relationship just happens. It wasn't until later in my career that I sought out mentors to discuss specific career plans." All the mentors he's had along the way are proud of his accomplishments and never felt competitive with him because they were much more senior than he.

Master the Informal Network As Well

Bruce Colligan, who is fifty-four years old, spent nearly three decades at AT&T as a vice president in Operations and Human Resources for Business Customer Care, Small Business Markets, and the Communication Services Group. Despite the many formal mentoring programs at AT&T, Colligan, who is white and saw how the dynamics of mentoring programs affected minority candidates, recommends that corporate employees "develop strong informal mentors. Having someone outside your reporting chain as a mentor brings vitality, a fresh viewpoint, and cross-pollination. Further, if you're hired in midcareer in a vice president–type job, you'll trigger enmity in many internal candidates who were seeking your job." Hence, going outside of your area is the wise course of action. In his corporate experience, formal mentoring programs can be useful, but often are rigid, bureaucratic, and obligatory. Informal mentors, he suggests, are often of much better value and influence.

Casting a Wide Net

Limiting yourself to the formal mentoring program would be far too narrow. Colligan suggests that ambitious minorities cast a wide net when searching for a mentor. When you attend a meeting, try to identify who the rising stars are. Often these people will come across as cocky, assured, and demonstrative, no matter what their level is. In fact, Colligan suggests that the minority candidates volunteer to participate in task forces throughout the firm. At these task forces, you'll have opportunities to work on joint programs with many senior and midlevel executives in different areas. That expands your network and opens possibilities for your next job. Making sure senior executives recognize your contribution is another must-do. The more you can impress them with your drive and enthusiasm, the more options you will have to choose a second or third mentor and position yourself to advance.

Vying for the Formal Mentoring Network

Asked what most companies look for in determining who is selected for their fast-track mentoring programs, Colligan replies, "The strongest candidates, the ones who display core competencies, and who demonstrate strong leadership skills." Often it's employees who impress several people in the organization, not just their boss or people in their business area. Ultimately performance is your admission ticket into the company's structured mentoring program and helps secure an informal mentor.

Choose a Mentor by Making Connections

When Bruce Colligan was interviewed for a job by John Legere, then a senior executive at AT&T and currently president of Global Crossing, he noticed a print of a runner by Leroy Neiman on his wall and asked if Legere ran. Legere said he was a jogger and marathon runner. Colligan had recently competed in a triathlon, and that connection may have contributed to his landing the job and snagging Legere as one of his key mentors during his AT&T career. "Look for connections. Try to find something personal. A book, a print, anything that connects and links you," Colligan encourages. Having Legere as his mentor catapulted Colligan on his ascent through AT&T. It led to his participating in AT&T's fast-track "Leadership Continuity" program and contributed to his being named a third-level manager. "Legere gave me the drive, supplied me with the skills, appointed me to task forces, and offered me advice," he says.

Choose the Rising Star

Raised in Mexico, forty-three-year-old Luis Nunez started working at Kellogg's in 1985, became a midlevel manager, and worked there until 1997. At age twenty-two, Nunez started working with Carlos Gutierrez, a general manager in Mexico. From the very beginning, Nunez says, Gutierrez had an aura of success. "He encouraged everyone to be better; he made you feel you were the best at what you were doing," Nunez says. Nunez considered Gutierrez to be one of his informal mentors. Gutierrez, who started as a cereal salesman in Mexico, kept moving up the corporate ladder and was named CEO in 1997. He was for many years the only Hispanic CEO of a Fortune 500 company, before he was named commerce secretary in 2004.

What did Nunez learn from him? "Gutierrez taught me about leadership, both explicitly in what he said and by observing his actions," he says. Gutierrez also gave Nunez the go-ahead to develop All Bran in Mexico. What can we learn from Nunez's selecting Gutierrez as his informal mentor? Look for natural leaders; choose mentors who will stretch your talent. Seek out a rising star who will move up the corporate ladder, and if he has confidence in your abilities, he will choose you for leadership positions.

Gracefully Choosing a New Mentor and Ending Your Current Relationship

Sometimes the mentor-mentee relationship goes sour. No matter how much you try, the mentor and you just don't hit it off. The chemistry is not there or trust doesn't develop. Sometimes the falling-out stems from the mentor being obligated to participate in the program but having too much on his or her plate. Sometimes the mentor is threatened by the mentee. You have the MBA, and he or she doesn't. You are more outgoing, a better communicator, and the mentor envies you. Extricating yourself from a sour mentoring relationship isn't easy. You don't want to offend the mentor, and you don't want to be stigmatized as someone who isn't a team player.

To extricate yourself gracefully, you can let the relationship fade and not contact the mentor, or you might seek out projects in other areas, which may lead you to find a new mentor. You might express your appreciation of the mentor's help by saying, "Thanks for your feedback and comments. It's been very helpful. I'm sure I'll be asking you for advice in the future" as you lessen the relationship and ease your way out gracefully.

Seeing Things from the Mentor's Viewpoint

Understandably, self-interest motivates people in corporations. Typically, the mentor derives a benefit from working with you, even if participating in the program is a way to give back to the company, or you'll find quickly that the monthly luncheon will turn into the semi-annual phone call.

Furthermore, in formal mentoring programs, the mentor's compensation could be affected by mentoring you. Her performance evaluation may include a judgment based on mentoring you. Hence, there's a lot at stake for your mentor.

If the mentoring is informal, and performance evaluations aren't involved, there still must be a payoff for the mentor. The mentor has to feel that grooming you will be considered a feather in her cap, shine positive light on her, and boost her standing in the company. So while you should consider how the mentoring relationship will help you move up, you also have to consider helping the mentor along the way.

Balancing the Mentor and Your Manager

Working in a corporate environment, a federal agency, or a large nonprofit involves constantly juggling conflicting demands at once. What if your manager gives you advice, and your mentor offers conflicting advice? How do you handle and balance them? What if your informal mentor tells you something that goes against what your formal manager says? If the informal mentor gives you advice, you have to make sure it's clandestine, not disclosed to your manager. If the advice is part of the formal program, you have to balance out what you think is best, without betraying any confidences.

Avoiding Political Minefields

Mentors and managers can try to use knowledge that you gained in mentoring sessions to their own advantage. Why is your manager pumping you for information about what your mentor, a senior manager in another business, is doing? It may help your manager understand where the company is headed. But how do you maintain your integrity and not divulge any confidences? You have to avoid being totally forthcoming, which can damage your reputation. Withholding information isn't lying; it's operating from a strategic viewpoint. Balance being honest with your manager and honest with your mentor. Ask your mentor whether information being told to you is between the two of you or can be made public. Don't get trapped in divulging information, which can damage your mentor. Conversely, your mentor may question you on what your manager and business area are doing. Again, avoid falling into any minefields, and release only information that you know can be publicized, and not politicized.

I counseled one midlevel executive at a major financial-services company who was very involved in a mentoring program. He was trapped in his area, so his mentor filled him in on many aspects of his company's business that he wasn't privy to. He was a rising star whose mentor was helping him advance. But he encountered a colleague who wanted the same promotion that he sought. He eventually gained the promotion, and out of pettiness belittled her, reinforcing that he had got what she had wanted. However, he did not know whom he was dealing with. She reported what he had done to her mentor, who was higher in the corporate food chain than his rabbi. Her mentor reported his behavior, which led to his losing his job. His rising star faded, and eventually he left the financial-services company, proving that politics must be played all the time, even among mentors.

When Mentoring Is Operating on All Cylinders

Mentors serve as navigational guides. Based on their experience in the company's culture, they can help you avoid the land mines, explain which behaviors are most rewarded in the company, and appoint you to a task force so that you can meet senior managers outside of your business area. The mentor can share what the marketing officer is looking for, or which area will provide you with a springboard to success.

When you and your mentor are in sync, enjoy each other's company, trust each other, and develop a strong rapport, mentoring can be one of your springboards to success. It can cover the wide spectrum of what it takes to advance, including improving your performance, knowing what skills to focus on, networking so your mentor introduces you to senior and middle managers, and recognizing what land mines to avoid. Your mentor can short-circuit any potential mistakes, guide your next move, and fine-tune your career strategic blueprint.

Choosing the Ultimate Godfather

When you look at the minority employees who have skyrocketed up the corporation, two factors stand out: their performance and their mentor. Only artists do things alone. Corporate professionals must depend on senior leaders to identify their talent, guide them through the minefields, and help them advance. It's almost as if you're climbing Everest and need a Sherpa to assist you. With the assistance of the most powerful godfather and based on the most superior performance, you can surmount those obstacles and succeed.

Action Steps

Many minority candidates sit back and wait for mentors to find them, anoint them as rising stars, and identify them as the firm's bright, talented managers of the future. But often that call never comes, and the minority candidates wait like a shipwrecked sailor on a raft, hoping to be rescued. Rather than sit back and be passive, reach out and find a mentor or several mentors; don't wait for them to find you. Here are action steps that can best secure your identifying the right mentors:

- If you're asked, join the company's formal mentoring program, gain as much from it as possible, but use it as a launching pad. Finding multiple mentors will heighten your chances of moving up the ranks.

- Find your own mentors. You don't need to rely on the company's structured mentoring program. Like Carlos Valle, you can establish your own mentor or mentors through your own personal connections, charisma, and relationships.

- Don't stop when you've developed your first mentor. Strive to find multiple mentors, each of whom may play a different role for you.

- Use your external contacts to find mentors outside of the company. Attend industry conferences and join alumni organizations to identify mentors who can advise you from outside the company.

- Spend as much time identifying the right mentor as you would buying a new auto. Try to pinpoint who are the rising stars in your company and find a way to meet them and become associated with them. The success that most minorities have had advancing in corporations is attributable to having a senior manager who believed in them.

- Select a mentor who will expand your thinking and your network, rather than satisfy your comfort level. Since most senior executives are Caucasian men, you'll learn more from someone with better contacts and superior political and strategic skills.

- Choose a mentor who is looking out for your best interests, helps you to navigate the company, enhances your connections, or appoints you to task forces.

- Once you've chosen a mentor who can help you navigate the company's minefields, maximize the relationship. Arrange lunches, periodic phone calls, half-hour meetings, or after-work trips to Starbucks. Ask questions. See if you can learn from him. Ask what projects or task forces he's working on and if you can be appointed to one of them.

- Monitor your mentoring relationships. If the relationship is going sour, identify new mentors. Avoid complacency. Even if you're aligned with a top performer, consider reaching out to other mentors who can teach you different skills or expand your network in other ways.

- View the mentoring relationship from the mentor's viewpoint, not just your own. What satisfaction is the mentor deriving from the relationship? What can you do to help the mentor? How can you connect your mentor to minority markets?

- Showing gratitude is one way to give back to your mentor. "I wanted to thank you for supporting me and helping me to advance. Your suggestions have been of critical importance to my development" is rather explicit. Mentors are people too and deserve recognition.

- Involve the mentor in your career strategic plan. What will it take to get you to the next rung? In order to become a vice president, what skills must you possess?

3

MAKING THE RIGHT CONNECTIONS— NETWORK, NETWORK, NETWORK

M OST MAJORITY PEOPLE have been networking their entire lives. Networking comes naturally to them. For many
majority people, it's part of their culture and upbringing. They grow
up a member of a country club, their parents attended Yale University or Bard College or USC, and friends introduce friends. Their
parents volunteer at the local Rotary Club or attend the annual benefit in town, which leads to knowing more people. If their parents'
best friend works at Bank of America, an introduction to the HR director opens the door for employment. Networking has its privileges.

But if you are a minority from a working-class family, your connections tend to be limited. Your parents likely didn't belong to a
country club or a profession, but grew up playing softball or basket-
ball in schoolyards. And that won't create many networking opportunities.

Many minority employees don't fully understand the benefits of
networking. It's as if they don't see the return on investment. They
fail to understand that networking yields concrete opportunities by

expanding the number of contacts, making connections, opening up doors, and finding out what possibilities are out there beyond their narrow circle of friends and colleagues.

Moreover, too many minorities see networking opportunities like attending conferences or panels as a time to have fun rather than a way to implement their strategic blueprint and advance their career. Attending these functions turns into fiesta time, involving drinking beer or margaritas with friends. Letting down one's hair and partying are ways to release energy and have fun, but networking requires focus, concentration, and hard work. Why let your majority counterparts use networking to leverage opportunities and advance their career while you're partying?

By networking, you're going to be adding to your career-advancement tool kit. Just as you've learned to use spreadsheets, improved your presentation skills, and added a host of other skills, you can add networking to your repertoire. It's a learned task, just like many others.

In the unwritten code about networking, majority people use it to get ahead and minorities often don't know how to be proficient at it. Learning the skills of networking can help you to level the playing field and provide an equivalent chance of moving up. The more adept you are at networking, the more you can use it to advance your career, find mentors, learn about job opportunities, and boost your skills.

Mistake #1: Thinking That Networking Is Beneath You

Too many minority professionals downgrade networking and overlook its many benefits. Rather than seeing its strengths of expanding contacts, feeling the pulse of their industry, and extending their reach beyond the limits of their company, many see networking as a waste of time. Others see it as "using people." They see it as equivalent to manipulating people, which goes against their religious or ethical beliefs, instead of seeing it as a quid pro quo—a mere reciprocal agreement between people. You help me and I'll help you. Moreover, networking creates a much wider net of acquaintances, colleagues, and contacts in your industry or firm. If you pooh-pooh networking and are reluctant to participate in it, you cut off one of the main avenues that will get you noticed, expand your connections, and open up possibilities in your career blueprint.

In the old days companies were loyal to their staff and didn't downsize, and most people worked for one company for thirty-five years and then retired. Networking wasn't all that important. But those days are gone. Networking exposes you to people at different companies who may help you connect with the right person when it's time to move on. Like mentoring, networking adds to your repertoire and tool kit and helps achieve your strategic plan. Without it, you're trying to traverse the Atlantic Ocean on a raft alone—no easy task.

Mistake #2: The Willy-Nilly Approach

I've observed many minority employees who treat networking as if it were the same as going for a drink after work. They attend a conference, hand out a business card, drink some wine, and spend their time schmoozing with friends that they already know. Instead of attending the conference with a set plan, agenda, and purpose, they're content to have a good time, sit in on a panel, or aimlessly wander the conference. Rather than taking the time to meet people, make connections, and benchmark their career with enlightened employers, minorities often fail to take advantage of the opportunity to seize the day and network.

I encourage you to conduct due diligence on an event. Go to the organization's Web site; find out who will be attending and what the presentations will be; obtain last year's conference magazine; and determine before you attend whom you want to meet and what outcomes you want to leave the event with. If you leave with fewer than ten business cards and have not given out ten of your own, you have not taken maximum advantage of an opportunity.

Mistake #3: Acting Unprofessionally

You wear your blue jeans or fail to wear your jacket and tie, drink four glasses of wine, get tipsy, say inappropriate things, and then wonder why people haven't gravitated toward you. Acting unprofessionally at a conference is verboten. It makes a bad first impression and can damage your reputation, tarnish your name, and cancel out any benefits that come with networking. In order to move up the ranks, you need to be on top of your game at every moment and take advantage of every opportunity. A networking event is a critical time to make a name for yourself and toot your own horn without coming across like a rapacious salesman. If you use foul language and come across as coarse and crude, you have impaired your reputation and not achieved anything. Always act professionally; seize the opportunity of networking.

Mistake #4: Taking the Passive Way Out

At most conferences, I see many people who participate in the event, go through the motions, but never accomplish very much. It's as if they think showing up is enough. Let the record show that Maryanne

Johnson and Marty Smith attended the conference. Showing up isn't enough. You have to work the event, show enthusiasm, devise the game plan, have a script or synopsis that you can deliver crisply and concisely without feeling self-conscious. Don't attend and make it seem as if you're doing someone a favor by showing up. Make the most of the event; put your best foot forward and come prepared to hustle.

Mistake #5: The Party Syndrome

While ambitious employees treat a networking event as part of their job, the uninformed treat it as party time. Ready to party, they overindulge, spend time with only the people they already know, and see it as an opportunity to let loose. While they're imbibing, their majority counterparts enter the event with the single-minded focus of an athlete ready to compete and take the prize. Forget the party mentality and treat networking as an opportunity to build your career and achieve the next stage of your strategic blueprint.

Develop a Networking Game Plan

When I attended a conference organized by the National Medical Association (NMA), a consortium of over thirty thousand African American physicians, I approached it with a set outlook, just like a football coach who devises an effective game plan to win the championship. I researched who was attending, and learned that the then president of the association, Dr. Winston Price, had attended my alma mater, Cornell University. I contacted him beforehand so he could introduce me to other doctors, and developed a strategy of what I wanted to accomplish and whom I wanted to meet in hopes of introducing them to a pharmaceutical client for career opportunities. At the conference I entered with high energy and enthusiasm, met people at the cocktail hour, made more connections at dinner, worked the floor, and then hobnobbed at the after-dinner cocktail ball. I was focused not on drinking wine but on making connections. I did not attend the conference with a haphazard approach but knew exactly what my game plan was: to meet prospective candidates and potential clients, position myself as the CEO of a leading-edge executive search firm, and make numerous contacts by the time I left the conference.

By conference's end, I had exchanged twenty-five business cards with attendees. Within a day, I had prioritized the cards into three or four doctors that I wanted to call to meet for lunch or breakfast, and three or four others that were possibilities for future client introductions.

Networking, like mentoring, adds another facet to your tool kit. Advancing up the corporation is such a complicated task that it entails a multilayered and multipronged approach. You need the mentors to help you navigate the company, and the more you can network, the more you open possibilities beyond the company you work for.

Operating on a Level Playing Field

Many minority employees complain that their majority counterparts have all the advantages: the connections, the Ivy League or other top-tier college, the elite suburban private school, and the golf club membership. Networking levels the playing field. If whom they know catapults people through the corporation, here's your opportunity to catch up and get one step ahead of your majority colleagues. Through your own initiative you can meet rising stars, leaders of organizations, senior managers, and peers (who could be moving up the ladder and bringing you with them) at other companies. Further, networking at your own company can help identify the decision makers who will determine whether or not you're promoted.

Achieving those connections doesn't come easy. It takes doing your homework, reaching out to other people, coming to events with a game plan, knowing what the organization is about, and familiarizing yourself with current trends in your industry so you can establish yourself as knowledgeable. You must also appear at these events with great energy and confidence. If you convey apathy, you won't make the connections.

What networking offers most of all for minority employees is exposure. While majority people can gain exposure by their connections or golf club membership, minority employees need a platform, and networking can fill that void. The more confident you feel at networking, the more you can showcase your strengths and experience when you meet senior leaders at conferences or events.

If you've written your strategic blueprint and constantly refer to it, networking can help speed up realizing it. Networking exposes you to more people within your company and stretches your outlook by enabling you to meet people outside of your company.

Networking Comes in Many Flavors

One benefit of networking involves making internal connections. Joining an African American, Hispanic, or women's affinity group at your company introduces you to many new people in the firm. You'll meet people on your level, on a level below yours, and senior vice presidents above you. At some of the events, speakers will discuss how to get ahead at the company, and at other events, you'll meet vendors, which will enable you to benchmark your progress against people at other companies.

In addition to your company's affinity groups, scores of ethnic professional organizations have emerged, which can be of enormous help in networking. In the engineering field, organizations such as the Society of Hispanic Engineers, the National Society of Black Engineers, and the National Council for Minority Engineers hold conferences, establish task forces to explore trends, try to attract more minorities into the profession, and trigger a wealth of opportunities for fast-track minority employees who want to meet new people and strengthen their expertise outside of their company. Equivalent organizations in other fields are easy to track down via Google or through other people in your firm.

Sometimes the most beneficial outcomes will arise from networking organizations that do not have the cachet of the better-known ones. Networking organizations such as the National Association for Multi-Ethnicity in Communications hold forums on multicultural marketing, and organizations like Business Network International, local Five O'Clock Clubs for recently downsized staff, or local chambers of commerce can yield extensive contacts.

Besides tapping the company's affinity organization, look for internal networking opportunities within your company. Sometimes attending special meetings and events, or joining the company's book club or bowling team, can lead to connections that can help you in innumerable ways. For example, when Lucent Technologies holds an all-day strategy session on the latest products it's introducing in the market, it can serve as an opportunity to meet people in other areas and explain how you can contribute to marketing this new product.

Also consider networking opportunities outside of your company held by your alumni association. When I started to participate in the Cornell Alumni Association, it led to my being named president of the Cornell Latino Alumni Association. In that capacity, I met many up-and-coming Latino executives, and then was named to Cornell's Trustee Council, a group of 350 Cornellians who serve as ambassadors to the university on various issues. At one Trustee Council event, I met and got to know Supreme Court justice Ruth Bader Ginsburg and Sandy Weill, the former CEO of Citigroup. All of those connections started with my joining the general Cornell alumni group and then intensifying my involvement.

But networking doesn't have to be executed in only formal gatherings. Just as you can take advantage of the formal mentoring program or develop your own informal mentors, the same is true of networking. You can meet people in the corporate cafeteria or the company's fitness center, and use those connections to form your own networking team. Start thinking about forming your own networking team who can assist you in moving up and meeting the right people. As we'll discuss later, the informal network can be at least as powerful as more established groups.

Using Networking to Get Ahead

When Connie Simons, fifty-three years old, joined Avon Products Inc. as an administrative assistant in 1979, she knew little about networking. "Back then, I shied away from networking. It's not my personality to introduce myself at events. I'm just not that aggressive," she admits. But as the years progressed, Connie saw that being a dedicated hard worker who got outstanding performance appraisals wasn't helping her realize her goal of becoming a manager. So she decided to network.

When she started seeing some of her peers advance while her career stalled, she says, she "started to realize that networking was important. I needed to talk and find individuals who had influential positions and communicate to them what my career aspirations were. I realized that doing a good job wasn't enough. No one knew that I wanted to advance." In short, she needed to toot her own horn because no one would tap Connie Simons on the shoulder to ask her to be a manager unless she networked effectively and asserted herself.

First she joined the Black Professionals at Avon (BPA), an affinity organization. At the BPA, she started meeting other influential African Americans whom she could rely on, use as a resource, and ask questions, and who could help identify the influential senior managers at Avon that would help her advance. Her involvement in the BPA "enlightened me to how powerful networks can be, how networking allows individuals to open up career opportunities, and find other people who will support you and your development." Prior to networking, she felt "excluded" at Avon. It was Connie Simons alone trying to move up, and it's difficult to climb the mountain solo. Through networking she identified people who believed in her, and each played a role in her ascent.

Develop Your Own Informal Network

The way to get ahead is to "develop your own network at the company," Connie Simons learned. Starting with her involvement in the affinity group, she identified four people at Avon who served as Simons's networking group. One African American senior manager served as a mentor and encouraged her to develop a strategy to advance, explaining that she couldn't expect to be named a manager in human resources just because she came in early and worked hard. A white manager helped her see that she had to take risks in order to move up, expand her networking, meet more people at Avon, and let them explicitly know that she wanted to become a manager. A Latino manager stressed that she had to educate herself, expand her skills set, see what skills a manager required, and make sure that she possessed all of them. Another African American woman boosted Simons's confidence and let her know that she had the skills and expertise to advance.

Networking permitted Simons to remove her blinders and get out of being locked into one business area. Until she started networking, she figured that hard work and concentrating only on her job would be sufficient to move up. Ignored and slighted, while others were promoted, she realized she had to call attention to herself and reach out beyond her limited business group. Through her networking, she learned what opportunities were available at Avon and was able to stress her own managerial potential. Networking taught her to define her skills, communicate her strengths to others, and meet the influential people who could promote her. Her networking group helped her identify the leaders she needed to meet at various meetings.

She learned through networking that she could package herself differently or present herself in a way that positioned her more effectively to become a manager. Whenever she met people at networking events, sales conferences, and meetings, she let people know that she was an HR generalist who specialized in recruiting. She was positioning herself as an HR supervisor who had the right skills to be named a manager. When someone met Simons at one of these networking events, there should have been no doubt in his or her mind that Simons was an HR generalist who was managerial material.

Simons was named manager of Global Resources at Avon Products in the early 1990s. What enabled her to advance when so many other minorities either leave the corporation or get stalled in their career? It was networking that made the difference. As she puts it, "It was the influence of those individuals that supported my promotion. They got to know me, my skills, and helped me to communicate to others that I wanted to be a manager."

The more networking she did, the better she got at it. Her confidence level rose, and she began to feel more comfortable doing it. Once she learned the skill of networking, she used it when she left Avon and joined Cablevision, where she served as a manager of Corporate Staffing, and subsequently as a senior consultant with AA Smith & Associates, a management consulting firm. Ironically, the once reluctant networker now coheads a networking practice at Catalyst, a New York nonprofit research and advisory organization that is dedicated to women advancing in business.

Ultimately, what effect did networking have on Simons's career? "Networking was my strategy to help advance my career. Networking was my success strategy. It expanded opportunities for me, formally and informally," she says. It created a platform for her that allowed her to showcase her strengths, which led to her being named manager.

Be Upbeat and Gregarious When Networking

Personally, I like introverted people. They can be of strong moral character and wonderful people, who tend to be a bit shy and self-effacing. But when it comes to networking, shy and introverted people don't win the prize. Succeeding at networking usually requires a more outgoing, gregarious personality. If you're naturally introverted, you need to tap something in you, like an actor playing a role, which enables you to be more outgoing, upbeat, and enthusiastic.

When attending an event, make sure you've had a good night's sleep; avoid overindulging in food or liquor, which usually tires you out; and come to the conference with considerable energy. You'll need to tap that energy to get out there, work the floor, be positive about yourself, focus on what you want to accomplish. As I said, come to the conference with a plan of what you want to say and how you want to come across, and make sure your tone is enthusiastic and upbeat.

Making the Most of Your Opportunities

At these events, many people are trying to make connections, including many of your colleagues and people at other companies. In order to meet enough people, ferret out the people who will help you, and make connections, you must be relentless, persistent, and tenacious. Networking effectively requires a total focus on accomplishing your goals, maintaining your energy, and making sure you've made the most of your opportunity.

Crafting Your Pitch

Networking events are often free flowing and informal, unlike a meeting where someone delivers a PowerPoint presentation. On the one hand, you can't prepare a five-minute speech that you want to deliver to someone you meet, which comes across as canned and artificial. Yet, you can't approach a networking event without any preparation either.

Connie Simons met with one of her advisers on her networking team and developed her own distinctive communication plan. Simons first took a step back and asked herself where she wanted to be in five years (her strategic blueprint), and then crafted a pitch to explain where she wanted to be. She emphasized her HR skills and recruiting background, since she supported Avon's nonexempt employees (staff level who are not managers) in the corporate office. "I was seen by the right people because my network led me to be seen by senior leaders within HR," she says. This made the difference.

I recommend jotting down several bullet points that summarize what you want to say to someone. "Hi, Ken Roldan, CEO of Wesley, Brown & Bartle, a national executive search firm with an over thirty-year history of positioning top talent in corporate America at multiple levels and multiple functions. We pride ourselves on our ability to court the passive job seeker who falls below the corporate radar screen." That intro is snappy, gives a person a sense of what I do, and is not too heavy-handed. And I'll change what I say to different people. So you're walking a line between being prepared and yet not sounding canned, and still being lighthearted and spontaneous about things.

"Networking Was Essential to Staying Alive"

When Bill Davis, who spent twenty-eight years working for Southern Bell Company, which turned into AT&T and later Lucent Technologies, started working in customer service in 1972, he got his job through networking, without even realizing it. As an undergraduate at North Carolina State, he started a minority recruitment program. He befriended the college's career placement officer, who helped him get an interview and land that initial job at Southern Bell in Charlotte. "Honestly, I knew nothing about networking," he admits.

As his career progressed and he moved up the ranks, he quickly learned that "networking was essential to staying alive." When he was starting out in customer service, his team was very close and had summer outings at the beach house of a district manager. Davis attended the meetings and observed how a majority colleague, Tom, played golf, hobnobbed, said all the right things, befriended everyone, and started to move up. At these events, Davis didn't play golf (he now does) and tended to stay off on the side and observe. While Davis's career stalled, he watched Tom start gaining promotions.

Davis, like many African Americans, thought schooling was the key to success. He tried to operate "smarter" (in his words) than everyone else, yet saw Tom advancing while he didn't. "I found out that being connected was more important than trying to be smarter," Davis says.

Master Informal Networking

While Davis was working at AT&T, he joined the African American affinity group. He attended meetings and networked with other employees, and found it helpful but limiting. In his view, formal networks offer modest opportunities for fast-trackers. "The real ball game is played in informal networks," he says.

The first thing he advises ambitious minority employees to do in order to start networking effectively is figure out the main specialty that they offer the corporation. Once you've identified what your specialty is, which is in fact branding yourself, you then can form informal networks and offer your skills.

For example, at Southern Bell, Davis was making a name for himself as coming into projects as a change agent. When projects needed to be overhauled, Davis would reengineer or reconfigure them and started building his reputation around this theme. When he started networking informally, he'd say to a senior manager, "If this operation is running smoothly, don't hire me. But if you need a change agent, I'm your man." Then he started telling vice presidents of sales and service that he was interested in becoming a general manager.

Another critical networking skill that Davis learned was seeking out the influential people, the decision makers. "Seek out the people that are in the positions that you desire. Get to know them and ask them how they got there. People at the top are usually willing to talk because no one asks them questions," he says.

Networking can also enable you to discover the land mines that are sprinkled along your corporate career path. When Davis was working on a job at Southern Bell with eight or nine other district managers, someone in his informal network clued him in that he was alienating two of the district managers. He focused on patching up those relationships, which allowed him to complete the job. "Networking can provide access to information, and tell you when you're in trouble or about to get into trouble," he says.

In 1992, when the Democratic National Convention was being held in New York at Madison Square Garden, Davis told a vice president that he was available as a change agent to manage AT&T's telecommunications. The vice president declined Davis's suggestion, saying that he needed an operations expert for the role. But when setting up telecommunications at Madison Square Garden encountered major snafus, the vice president called Davis and named him the manager of the project. "I was good at managing change and at informal networking," Davis says, which contributed to his being named a division staff manager at AT&T in 1998.

After leaving Lucent Technologies in 2000, he formed his own eponymous consulting firm, based in Raleigh, North Carolina, that builds networks among people and businesses. One underlying aspect of effective networking is that everything is reciprocal, he suggests. "It's all about giving back. You give to people who you know will give back to you," he says.

Succeeding at the Conference or Event

The more you can personalize dealings with people at any conference, the more successful you will be at networking events. Focus on one person at a time. What I find most irritating and troubling is meeting someone at an event who is talking to me but checking out the floor, figuring out whom he will speak to next, and sizing up the room. But what he is doing is not paying attention to the person he's conversing with.

Make each person feel special. For the duration of that five-minute interchange, focus on that one person, who works at Gillette, who attended Boston University and grew up in Baltimore. After you obtain her business card, jot down specifics that you remember as follow-up. The more you personalize and make each person feel special, the more leverage you can gain from these networking opportunities.

Further, as author Malcolm Gladwell described in his best-selling book *Blink,* a first impression goes a long way toward determining another person's viewpoint and attitude toward you, and is often indelible. Make sure you dress appropriately (and not provocatively), look the person in the eye, shake his hand with some zest, and focus on him, not on the crowd. Be upbeat and personable and have a good time.

Practice, Practice, Practice

I've encouraged minority people who attend networking sessions to work the room. But at your first event, you may not feel comfortable enough to do that. Identify two or three people that you want to meet. Make sure you maximize those connections. Meet them and make a strong first impression. In addition, make sure you have a clear-cut agenda and plan of attack. That will ease your nerves and reduce your anxiety.

If networking makes you feel uncomfortable or you think you're not skilled at it, another option is to test yourself in a less pressured situation. Start volunteering at a nonprofit agency. Find a cause that motivates you—the local Boys and Girls Club, the Make-A-Wish Foundation, a church charity—and get involved. At the nonprofit functions, you can test out your networking skills in an area that won't directly affect your job climb. Still, you can test out meeting people, exchanging business cards, and making connections, which could lead to something work related at another time.

At Avon, says Simons, who was hesitant at first to network, her skills improved the more she networked. "I learned how to put it all together, and that enhanced my confidence level," she says. As her networking experience grew, she began to relax, and then she could speak easily about what she had accomplished at Avon when she met senior leaders in HR, who would be influential in promoting her.

Now that she has become an experienced networker, she can work the room at these events, meeting scores of people. But when you're first starting out, avoid trying to meet everyone. Instead, narrow your focus. If you're successful, that can boost your confidence. At your second event, focus on meeting five people, and then start thinking about expanding your net.

The more events you attend, the better you'll get at them. Practice and experience improve your skills. After your first event, ask yourself what you did well, and where you can improve. Practice those skills at your next event. The more you network, the more you'll improve your skills.

Dealing with Accents

Some minority people are self-conscious because they were born in Taiwan, Peru, or Jamaica and have an accent. If you find that people are having a difficult time understanding you, keep your conversations short and to the point. Having an accent is fine; there's nothing wrong with it. But don't go off into tangents. Keep your conversation concise, know exactly what you want to say, exchange business cards, and explain who you are.

Following Up

After you've made the connections, exchanged business cards, and forged a positive relationship, the time is ripe for following up. Usually I'll prioritize the contacts I've made, separating the deal makers from the influencers who can connect me to the decision makers, the power brokers, and others. I usually write a thank-you note explaining how I enjoyed meeting the person, and I may ask more specifically about meeting for breakfast or lunch. If it's a less influential contact, I may ask about meeting at a coffee bar or for a glass of wine.

In the thank-you note, try to add something personal. Make it lively. The pro forma thank-you note that says, "I enjoyed meeting you at the conference. I wanted to follow up with you" reads like a pitch letter from an insurance company and should be avoided. Mention something that was said; inject some personal detail in it. The follow-up letter shouldn't be canned but should say, for example, "I enjoyed meeting you at the conference and discussing what the keynote speaker, Jim Rogers, said about the role interactive marketing will play in the twenty-first century. I look forward to meeting with you again, either for an informal lunch or at the next conference."

At the luncheon, I'll ask the influencer if he can introduce me to Jim Floyd, the head of HR, who is doing the hiring. What's in it for your networking colleague? It's equivalent to why people opt to mentor. It gives him recognition if I can deliver a talented minority CFO to the corporation.

Avoiding the Five- to Seven-Year Trap

As previously stated, in their fifth to seventh year, many minority employees start getting the itch to leave their company. They start seeing their majority counterparts moving up, gaining the premiere assignments, using their connections, and passing them by while the minority employee languishes and feels trapped. Succeeding at networking offers one way to avoid falling into this quagmire.

Networking enables you to stay fresh in the marketplace by keeping tabs on which jobs are open and what trends are affecting your specialty. At one event you can learn that Intel is working on a new chip, or Merck is developing a new product, or Grey Advertising is exploring a new interactive Internet ad, all of which could interest you. If you stay siloed in your own company and don't know what's going on outside of the confines of your specialty, you'll remain trapped. By joining networking groups, organizations in your specialty, you'll learn of opportunities outside of your firm, connect to your strategic blueprint, and have more possibilities of finding jobs outside of your company.

Link Networking with Your Strategic Plan

Networking won't make things happen in and of itself. Your rising up in the corporation still depends on your performance, your finding a godfather, your multiple mentors, and your connections at the company. But networking can serve as a catalyst to open up doors. If your strategic plan says that in five years you'll be in charge of a marketing campaign, then networking should dovetail with that. Focus on meeting more decision makers in marketing who can make that happen.

Action Steps

- No matter what your personality, shy or gregarious, start networking on a small scale.

- Join an affinity group at your company. If you're a woman, African American or Latino, join one of the groups and start introducing yourself around. Participate in committees or conferences.

- Practice being upbeat and enthusiastic. Start exchanging business cards and see how connections made can help you.

- As Connie Simons did at Avon, take a risk and form your own networking team. Choose people who bring out different aspects of your personality and can connect you to the senior leaders who will be influential in promoting you.

- Seek out senior managers who can clue you in on what it will take to advance. Bill Davis suggests that informal networks often possess more clout and influence than being one of two hundred members of affinity groups.

- Create a punchy two-minute synopsis of who you are but keep it fresh and spontaneous as well. Don't turn it into a canned introduction.

- Brand yourself. Davis moved up by branding himself as a change agent and gaining several challenging assignments that advanced his career.

- During networking sessions, focus fully on the one person that you're engaged with. Concentrate on listening and getting to know the person, rather than scanning the room and seeing whom you can meet next.

- After a networking session, jot down significant details on the person's business card. For example: "Two years in HR at Lucent Technologies, likes to play golf, discussed Jack Welch's last book, *Winning*."

- Send follow-up e-mails or notes to people with whom you want to stay in contact with. Consider asking the prime influencers to lunch and see in what ways you can connect.

- Branch out beyond affinity groups. Start looking for professional groups to join in marketing, finance, or sales that you think could extend your network beyond your company.

- Do your homework at these events. Learn who will be speaking and see if you have any alumni connections. Choose someone who can make your life a little easier by introducing you around. Decide which panels you want to enroll in and whom you'd like to meet.

- After participating in several conferences, events, or workshops, start working the room. Set goals of exchanging five, then ten business cards.

- Create an "exchange program" with some of the people you network with. Consider whom you can introduce them to, and start thinking about whom you'd like them to connect you with.

- As you feel more comfortable, ramp up your involvement in networking groups. Consider participating in a panel at the annual conference, or even lending one.

- Tie your networking in with your strategic plan. What do you have to do to move to the next level, become a vice president, and get the next challenging assignment? What contacts at your company will get you there? If your ascension has stalled, what other options are out there for you?

- Let networking expand your horizons beyond your
  company. Don't stagnate and think that the world
  revolves around your business or division. See what other
  options are out there. Use networking to benchmark
  your progress.

4

MASTERING CORPORATE POLITICS

N OW THAT YOU'VE created the strategic blueprint, identi-fied your mentors, and developed your own network, you've positioned yourself to succeed. But there's a missing piece that is nec-essary to advancing up the corporate ladder: mastering corporate pol-itics. If you are not savvy and skillful in mastering corporate politics, you'll wind up stuck in your job, not moving up, and considering leaving corporate life to open a franchise, or enter the nonprofit or government sector.

One of the reasons minority corporate employees miss out on mastering corporate politics is their naïveté or obliviousness. Schooled on the belief that hard work and strong performance will lead to success, minorities ignore corporate politics. They fail to think strategically, and don't bother to impress their boss and the senior vice president. Viewing the corporate structure like one big chess game is essential to advancing. To truly succeed in corporate life, you often need to operate like a politician—you must appeal to various constituencies or stakeholders, including your boss, his or her boss, peers, subordinates, and customers. To advance, you need buy-ins and approvals from each stakeholder. If you antagonize a boss or those stakeholders who are involved in that chain of command, and leave a strong negative impression, you can damage, if not ruin, your chances of advancement.

Further, many minorities have been left out of the old boys' network, the traditional hobnobbing paths that result in getting to know senior managers on the golf course, at the local Rotary Club, in suburban communities, or in private schools. A number of minority employees are turning to golf schools to learn the game and advance their networking on the greens; but many start after a dozen years of corporate life and seeing white counterparts who aren't as hardworking or as smart advance through talking about their handicaps, attending one benefit and fund-raiser after another, and schmoozing over beer with senior managers. If you can't befriend senior executives in normal social endeavors, you need to find alternative ways to reach them, such as volunteering, joining task forces, or other corporate venues.

I've also detected too many minority employees who have a distorted self-image. Some consider themselves superior performers when in reality they are only mediocre. Others depend on what they are told in performance appraisals. Performance appraisals, when done right, can be helpful. Often with minority employees, they fail to tell the whole story, since companies are afraid of triggering lawsuits. Many minority employees never ask for true feedback and just go on their merry way thinking they're on the fast track. I strongly encourage you to tap into your formal and informal network to determine whether you're on the fast track or not. If you're not, ascertain how to get there.

Clinging to the illusion that they are irreplaceable at their company, some minority professionals think that their presence alone will launch their success. Ignoring corporate politics, they think that bravura and a strong personality will make them successful. Instead, they often antagonize superiors and alienate colleagues, and then get bitter and resentful when they get passed over. Or they will use racism and discrimination (which clearly exist) as excuses for why they're not being promoted! But what's really at work here is an inability to master corporate politics, not racism. Avoid the race card at all costs.

One way to improve your knowledge of corporate politics and acquire new skills is to be astute about your surroundings. More important, rely on your mentors and network. Ask your mentor how to read the corporate tea leaves, navigate the company's minefields, determine which people you need to impress and who the decision makers are, and learn what senior management is really looking for in terms of performance. Sometimes the qualities that lead to success, such as assertive behavior, increasing revenue, and thinking outside the box, aren't included in the company's mission statement, which reads more like something from a Boy Scout handbook.

Let's face the facts: corporate minority employees face obstacles moving up the corporate ladder that majority people don't. As you begin to climb the ladder and become a vice president, advancing to the level of senior vice president or managing director becomes more competitive, Darwinian, and cutthroat. And minorities face another major obstacle: majority power players don't like relinquishing power and often want to choose their successor, who often looks like them or is part of their inner circle. In order to advance, you have to outsmart, outmaneuver, and outperform your majority counterparts when playing the chess game.

Learning to play corporate politics involves maintaining positive relationships with everyone in the company. That's right, everyone.

The administrative assistant of a senior vice president who has learned that you were taking shortcuts can undermine your efforts and damage your reputation just as much as the senior executive can. Everyone at the company is a potential ally or enemy; hence maintaining positive rapport and treating everyone with respect are essential. Embracing collaborative work, possessing a good sense of humor, not taking yourself too seriously, involving the entire team in the task, and recognizing superior performance are all qualities that ensure maintaining positive relationships.

A chess master makes a move that sets up his next two plays: that's how you must operate in corporate politics. You have to be strategic, plan ahead, and recognize that joining a task force, which will mean additional work, will connect you with a senior leader who could be influential in promoting you. Identifying senior managers who can assist you, finding out what makes your boss tick, and figuring out the latest trend at your company are all part of being a strategic thinker.

Playing corporate politics also means rising to your maximum level of achievement. I've met too many minority employees who are extremely bright and talented, but who suffer from low expectations. One candidate told me, "I'll play the game, but I never wanted to win the prize." Isn't that like entering a tournament and saying you want to compete but don't care if you win or not? What she really meant was she wanted someone to anoint her as the brightest employee around, but didn't want to establish a connection with senior executives, do the hard work of networking, impress her bosses, or tie her goals in with the company's. She wanted someone to designate her as a star and move her up the ranks, without having to self-initiate. Corporate politics doesn't work that way. If you acknowledge corporate politics plays a role in success, play it to win and move up the ladder as high as possible.

Mistake #1: Avoiding Corporate Politics

Some minorities want to stay pure and think that playing corporate politics will sully their reputation or damage their soul (that's the language we use to explain why we won't play the game). Others decide that they are not skilled at company politics and just shun it. Others just opt not to play by a corporation's rules but want to make it by playing by their own beliefs. But politics is inextricably woven into the fabric of corporate life. Learning to play it, master it, and be skillful at it is as important as becoming competent in your job.

Mistake #2: Trying to Set the Rules of Corporate Politics

Rather than try to play corporate politics, some minority employees decide that they will make their own rules. Instead of pleasing their bosses and connecting with the company's goals, they decide to write their own script. They decide to do *what they want to do,* in lieu of meeting the company's goals, operating as a team player, or connecting with their superiors. Ultimately that go-it-alone strategy backfires and leads to the employee leaving the company and becoming a consultant.

If you can't play the game by their rules, try a small nonprofit organization, where the politics isn't as thick (there's always politics in every organization with two people or more). Working at a large, complex, multidivisional organization means getting involved in corporate politics—if you want to move up. But denying its existence or just not playing the game is like writing your ticket out of corporate life.

Mistake #3: Antagonizing the Wrong People

On your climb up the ladder, you never know who might help or hinder you along the way. The person who sat in the next cubicle, who was an ordinary salesperson, might well turn out to be the senior executive, CFO, or CEO of tomorrow. Hence, playing politics means maintaining positive relationships with everyone, including subordinates and immediate supervisors. One of my candidates moved up a notch, surpassed a colleague who was in competition for the same position, and needled her about his promotion. Two years later, she was named his manager and fired him the next day. She didn't forget who had belittled her, and evened up the score.

Mistake #4: Obliviousness of the Power Structure

In the 1960s, during a time of civil unrest, protestors sang "Power to the people" at demonstrations. But in corporate America, power rests in the senior executive corridor more than with the shareholders or company employees. To play corporate politics effectively, know who makes the influential decisions in your business, your sector, and the overall company. Learning what makes the power structure operate will help you marshal your forces and strategize effectively. The more you can impress the power brokers, the more you can secure your rising to the next rung of the corporate ladder and ensure a steady ascent.

Mistake #5: Being Defensive and Personalizing Everything

Often when minority employees get questioned, they turn defensive. Many minorities take criticism personally, as if they were being attacked. That defensiveness can deter their moving up the ranks. Many majority people take criticism in stride, bounce back, and act in a resilient way. My advice is to put racism and discrimination to the side. As minorities, we tend to be oversensitive and often get bent out of shape when criticized or questioned, which hurts our chances of moving up. Learn how to play the game. Don't take the criticism personally. Don't get flustered. And at all costs, don't use the race card. Focus on problem solving. Concentrate on outcomes and don't show any weakness.

Do Your Homework/Due Diligence

Where do you learn the intricate and unwritten rules of mastering corporate politics? You won't learn them from the company's mission statement, which talks about respecting other people and being team players and being the best (all of which are well and good but won't teach you corporate politics). You won't master the intricacies in an MBA program, where the emphasis is on boosting revenue and learning about financial statements. The onus is on you to perform your own due diligence.

One technique is to return to the informal network that you've been developing. Contact your alumni network and see who previously worked at IBM, Procter & Gamble, the Guggenheim Foundation, or wherever you're employed. Ask to meet with him or her and ascertain the real deal: what the corporation is seeking from its senior managers, and who is getting promoted and why. Does the company seek creative people, as GE has recently been stressing, designing new ways to boost revenue that can appeal globally to Third World countries, its largest emerging market (20 percent of its revenue stems from this market)? Does it want numbers people who only watch the bottom line? Does it truly want team players, since everything it does is collaborative? Do the aggressive advance or do the strategic get ahead? Do they come from P&L areas or marketing or both?

Tap your mentors as well. Besides helping you know which skills it takes to succeed, the mentor will show you where the land mines are. Does Whirlpool want outspoken people who can expand the company into new products, rather than yes people who rely on the status quo? Does Heinz look for creative people or operations people to choose as senior leaders? Because of scandals in the Big Four accounting firms, are ethical accountants the new trend?

Make Your Boss Look Good

The more you can please your boss, and help him or her move up and look good, the better you will position yourself for your promotion. It's a symbiotic relationship. You help your boss and your boss helps you. You're a team, and winning gets the payoff and rewards. Making your boss look good can take a variety of forms, including minimizing risk, introducing a new product, or raising performance statistics on customer satisfaction. Since the flavor of the month is constantly changing in business, your priorities have to adapt. One day it will be Six Sigma, the next day improving diversity numbers, the next day outsourcing to India, and the next day a return to ethics.

Strategizing to Master Corporate Politics

In the following pages, you'll read about a JPMorgan Chase vice president who was very skillful, kept moving up the corporate ladder, made one misstep, and failed in her quest to become a managing director; another senior executive who worked at PepsiCo, NBC, Dell Computer, Disney Corporation, and Mattel, who learned to find common interests with majority executives despite not being part of their inner circle; and a senior executive who moved between Xerox and nonprofit organizations and learned that outspoken African American women can trigger strong reactions in senior executives.

They mastered several critical points in order to advance. Mastering corporate politics stems from on-the-job experience and can't be learned from a textbook or graduate school classes.

In the pursuit of moving up, managing upward is paramount. While you have to establish positive relationships with peers and subordinates, senior managers will ultimately determine whether you are promoted.

In that pursuit, learn who the decision makers are and cultivate them. Don't think that establishing positive rapport with one or two, or with an influential human resources director, will be sufficient. Target each and every decision maker.

Learn to go after what position you seek and don't masquerade your ambitions. If you soft-pedal them, and expect a senior executive will read your mind, it can hamper your quest upward. Be explicit about what you want to accomplish while still focusing on your job responsibilities and achieving the company's goals.

Developing positive rapport with your colleagues is always important, but your ability to generate profit for the company, no matter what department you're in, may be a deciding factor in your advancement. Even HR directors are judged by how the employees they recruit perform and add to the bottom line.

Even if you're not part of the old boys' network, strive to feel accepted and reach out to majority people. Don't be satisfied operating as the young boy standing outside the fence, watching everyone else play hardball. If you want to advance, gaining acceptance will help trigger your moving up.

Think strategically. You won't move up overnight. But you need to create a plan of whom you need to impress, pursue challenging positions that will help you gain notoriety and recognition, and cultivate senior leaders who are the decision makers in your organization. Moving up won't occur by happenstance or because you're a hard worker who arrives each morning at eight o'clock. It will result from the strategic pursuit of a goal and winning the confidence of senior leaders.

Know the Players

When Paulette Mullings, forty-four years old, started her career at Chemical Bank in 1984 as a junior auditor, what she knew about corporate politics derived solely from what she had read in her college textbooks. "They taught us in school that if you worked at a Big Eight accounting firm, you were going to work your butts off, work long hours, and you had to be politically astute," says Mullings, who advanced to be a vice president at JPMorgan Chase before leaving the firm in 2005. The Jamaican native, who was educated in the United States, admits that her knowledge of corporate politics grew and developed from twenty years of work experience, transcending the minimal amount she had learned from her college textbooks.

To advance, Mullings learned, "you have to maneuver the land-scape and know the players. You have to know whom to talk to, at what point to talk to them, making sure you don't offend anyone who has influence and control." That art of tact and diplomacy is critical to moving up. Fast-trackers learn to speak their mind, yet in a way that doesn't offend or threaten anyone.

It's the whole package that helps put you in a position to advance, Mullings suggests. You have to look the part; that doesn't necessarily mean buying the most expensive suits, but wearing clothes with con-fidence, having presence when you enter a room, and even on casual days, wearing clothes that make you look professional and not ready to clean out the basement.

As stated in the previous two chapters, securing a mentor and de-veloping an informal network lay the foundation for moving up. Mullings's mentor, a senior manager in the general audit department at JPMorgan Chase, appointed her to task forces, which led to her working with many other senior managers. "You get involved in de-partment projects and activities. You ask for feedback on what kind of impact your work is having," she says. One project gained tremen-dous visibility for her department, which raised her profile.

Managing upward is paramount. "It's important to make sure you influence all the right players," she says. For example, Mullings had been named to the corporate-wide Diversity Committee, in which the chairman and the president of the firm participated. When an upcoming meeting was planned at headquarters, she called the head of her department, who was not on the committee, and told him where the meeting was being held. He managed to arrive on the floor fifteen minutes before the meeting started, and started hobnobbing with the CEO and president. "You give good information," the de-partment head told Mullings, thankful for the inside information and always ready to network and manage upward himself. That inside information endeared her to him, which strengthened her reputation in the department and cemented her boss's trust. Information is power, Mullings suggests.

Reading Between the Lines

Most corporate senior managers will not explicitly tell you "this is what you have to do to be promoted in this department. It doesn't work that way," suggests Mullings. Everything is told through subtext and clues. "People in high positions just don't say what's on their minds. Instead they give you clues," she says. The HR director hinted that Mullings had to join a task force and make an impact, which, thanks to her mentor, she did.

Further, Mullings says, "Most senior managers do not tell you directly what it takes to move up." While Mullings was told she was an outstanding performer, her senior managers also told her to network more in order to get closer to senior managers of influence. She says senior managers were always walking a fine line between not wanting to divulge confidences, that is, describing exactly what the other senior managers thought of Mullings, and desiring to be helpful. Hence, she had to read between the lines and flesh out more of what it would take for her to move up.

Build Your Résumé by Volunteering

Mullings volunteered at the Make-A-Wish Foundation, a nonprofit organization, which grants wishes to dying children, which also helped her meet people and increase her public profile. She met her mentor, who was on the board of the Make-A-Wish Foundation. "It's perceived as a positive in the firm to give back to the community. It's also an excellent place to network. Since I don't play golf, I had to find alternatives," she says.

Besides managing upward, Mullings emphasized getting along with everyone. "If many people on your staff complain to HR about you, it will damage your chances of moving up," she says. When a new head of the department was named, Mullings saw the department head's administrative assistant unpacking at six o'clock one evening and befriended her. Administrative assistants of senior managers can make or break your career by passing along information about you to their boss, so Mullings goes out of her way to befriend them. "Administrative assistants have a lot of influence," she says. "It's important to get along with everyone at all different levels."

After eight years as a vice president, Mullings wanted to advance to the next level, managing director. That was the promotion that she sought and did everything in her power to attain. Yet when the decision came, she didn't get it, despite serving on task forces, impressing her direct manager, and gaining the respect of many senior managers. Why not?

Mullings says there were eight people on the executive committee of her department that made promotion decisions. She gained the respect of her direct manager and the human resources director and figured that those two would be her champions and influence the committee to promote her. She maintained positive relationships with the others. But she overlooked one senior manager on the committee, whom she had minimal dealings with. She later found out that he had not been impressed with her work and may have felt slighted that she, over a prolonged period, had never reached out to him. He spoke out against her and influenced the human resources director to question her promotion, which was denied. "I overlooked him, and that led to my downfall. It's important to identify all the major players," she says.

Making Your Own Case

After not being promoted, and after a new department head had settled in and changed the way the department was run, Mullings left JPMorgan Chase and is now an audit director at the American International Group (AIG) (hired by her mentor, who had also left JPMorgan Chase). Is there something she would have done differently in terms of playing corporate politics? The HR director told her that she "didn't make enough noise." By that she meant that Mullings needed to make a stronger case with each person on the executive committee for why she deserved to be promoted. Actions don't always speak for themselves. Without being overly pushy, Mullings should have made a stronger case that her actions and experience warranted her being named a managing director.

What does it take for a minority to move up the ranks? Mullings replies, "Perseverance, possessing the entire package of smarts and the right look, learning to be tactful, getting involved in projects that make an impact, and getting noticed. Networking and, of course, performance are key." She describes a former colleague, who is African American and was named a senior vice president, as someone who worked hard in his job and at playing golf. Ironically, she thinks his golf game added to his expertise as a deal maker. As demonstrated in the next chapter, he had to be a top performer, but his social skills added to his tool kit. He always played golf with senior managers, and loved both talking about the game and deal making over a beer at the clubhouse. He had, as Mullings says, the entire package. He walked with a certain cockiness, impressed his bosses, knew his stuff, but most of all, excelled at networking. He advanced because of his hard work and politicking.

What I see frequently in my executive search experience is minority employees who want to move up, but don't want to let anyone know they want to advance. Instead, they want senior executives to read their mind. It's as if they want to be anointed as a senior vice president without putting themselves on the line. If you want to move up, you have to let people know explicitly that you want the senior position. Just as Mullings learned that she had to make a case for herself, you have to initiate, go for it, and make a case for yourself. Everything you do, every building block that you put in place, helps achieve your goal. And that entails playing corporate politics in an ever-increasing number of concentric circles—your specific business, the larger business, the company—and networking externally.

Gaining Access to Power and Influence

Having served as vice president of Leadership, Staffing, Development, and Diversity for a leading financial-services company from 2000 to 2003, Dr. Amy A. Titus has seen how corporate politics play out behind the scenes in the senior executive corridors. Based on her observation, she attributes moving up the ladder to three major factors: (1) access to power, controlling and amassing it; (2) controlling and gaining information, the sooner the better; and (3) accruing influence. No matter what your level or job, if you can position yourself so that your actions and comments can influence decision making, then you're poised to move up. All three factors—gaining power, having access to information, and exerting influence—are cornerstones of playing politics, she says. Titus says you gain that access by volunteering for assignments, joining task forces, reaching across businesses and participating in committees, and engaging in conferences, where you meet senior managers at your company and others.

Getting the Plum Assignments

The most expeditious and effective way of gaining power and influence, Titus observes, is through "getting the plum assignments. Everything revolves around securing those assignments. That's where climbing the ladder and playing politics pay off." Those assignments differ from company to company, and vary as the company's priorities change. In one division it may be involvement in mergers and acquisitions, often one of the most lucrative and visible assignments; but it could also be a change project that reorganizes the company. Use your mentor and your networking to ferret out which plum assignments are emerging and then make sure you get them. Be aggressive. Position yourself effectively. Make sure you do your homework and are extraordinarily competent. Gaining that plum assignment is the fastest way to ensure moving up, Titus says.

Because of the Internet, changing markets, intensified competition, and the global marketplace, everything in business has sped up. What's a priority today becomes passé tomorrow. Figuring out what's the next great trend or profit generator is another skill that helps a minority employee move up. Because minorities are often outsiders, this status may be to their advantage. Reality television, DVD players, satellite radio, radio frequency identification tags, whatever industry you're involved in, if you can see the next business revenue producer, take a lead role, and get that plum assignment, you can stay one step ahead of the competition.

Overcome the Five- to Seven-Year Freeze

In her twenty years of experience in consulting and HR management, Titus, who is in her forties, has seen scores of talented minority employees whose careers stall after five to seven years. How can they play corporate politics effectively to reenergize and revive their careers? Finding another mentor is essential. Find a mentor two rungs up who can provide that career-making assignment, reveal current company information, and help you increase your influence, she suggests. "Become aggressive in a nonaggressive way," she says; start arranging lunches and asking senior managers for coffee, while not coming on like gangbusters.

Judge Everyone's Character

Reading each senior executive's character and determining what he or she is seeking in terms of competence can help you succeed. Some senior managers see everything in terms of problem solving. If that is their dominant approach, taking a problem-solving approach yourself will impress them. Others are focused on employee satisfaction. If your employees are satisfied, then your customers can be retained. Hence, focus on employee satisfaction. But all of this analysis depends on judging the character and values of the boss or senior manager and then adopting a game plan that will yield results.

Know Whom to Trust and Mistrust

Over the last fifteen years, well-traveled forty-seven-year-old Anthony W. Gilliard has been a human resources manager at PepsiCo for five years, spent three years each in HR at NBC, Dell Computer, and the Disney Corporation, and worked at Mattel for a year. He has seen how the executive suites operate and how senior executives are selected, and learned about the unwritten rules of corporate America.

His major advice to talented minorities eager to move up is, "Look, listen, and trust the right people. Be careful about whom you put your trust in." He describes himself as an "African American man who, even though he's a nice, supportive guy, isn't invited to the parties and the golf courses. They become intimidated because I'm not the white guy who plays golf with them." He has hosted several parties with his wife at his Los Angeles home, but has rarely been invited to parties at the homes of other senior executives. While he says that most senior executives are not overtly racist, he finds a social disconnect that prevents whites and African Americans and other minorities from forming strong bonds.

Having had considerable success and risen to the level of HR manager at Fortune 500 companies, Gilliard says that minorities need to maintain an open and accepting attitude toward their majority colleagues. "You never have a negative attitude, unless someone gives you a reason to," he says. Yet he suggests that minorities have to listen and constantly observe their majority colleagues in order to determine whom they can trust.

For example, at PepsiCo, Gilliard had been cordial with a senior white executive who had a Harvard MBA. At a diversity-training program that they both participated in, the level of discourse at the session was heating up. At one point, the majority executive blurted out, "Why is it that all the blacks always stick together in the cafeteria?" Frustrated by his obliviousness, Gilliard asked him if he had ever invited an African American colleague to join him at lunch, which led to a rather tense moment, and an answer of no.

On the other hand, Gilliard befriended a host of majority colleagues who genuinely tried to get to know him and with whom he established strong ties. "You can tell who are genuine human beings who take a personal interest in you. They were interested in getting to know me as Tony, and it didn't matter to them if I was African American or not," he says. Gilliard suggests that you think critically about your majority counterparts, and learn which majority managers and colleagues you can trust, and whom to be cautious with.

Find Commonalities

Because the odds are strong that as a minority you weren't raised in a privileged, suburban, country club environment, you hail from a different culture than most senior executives. Hence, what you need to do is find commonality, shared interests that bring you and the majority executives together to form bonds and transcend differences. For example, when Gilliard was at PepsiCo, he met a senior executive in HR who hailed from a background very different from his. But early on Gilliard discovered that the senior executive loved rooting for the New York Giants, which matched Gilliard's enthusiasm for the Dallas Cowboys. Despite their rooting for rival teams, their love of football connected them and led to a close friendship and business relationship.

Since that majority senior executive managed the succession planning at PepsiCo, he played an instrumental role in helping Gilliard advance. "Finding common ground" between men and women, people of different nationalities and ethnic groups, can be critical in moving up, Gilliard says. Furthermore, you need "sponsorship," he says, another term for a mentor or networking group.

Ensure a Feeling of Comfortability

Gilliard describes what must go on between a minority employee and senior executives as a "good fit. They have to feel comfortable to sit at the table with you. They have to know you speak their language, know how to assert yourself in corporate ways, and can generate results." You also need to become familiar with as many senior executives across the organization as possible.

When Gilliard worked for PepsiCo in Dallas, a majority senior manager once took him aside and told him that he was producing results but had to get himself known throughout the organization. "You're good at what you do. But you go to L.A. on business, do your business, and come home. Nobody knows you there." Based on this feedback, Gilliard started extending his trips to L.A.; he began to arrange dinners with senior executives and get himself known. As more senior executives know you and become familiar with you, it boosts your name recognition and heightens your chances of getting promoted, he says.

Adapt to Each Corporate Culture

Every corporate culture creates its own norms and expectations for moving up, Gilliard suggests. At PepsiCo, in every job you had, whether it was in marketing, sales, or human resources, you were judged by how your work impacted sales. If you were in HR and hired the leading manager for sales in the Eastern District, your profile was raised and you were destined to advance. If you hired poor performers, the senior manager told you during the performance-appraisal process how you had to improve.

In the entertainment business at Disney Corporation, everything revolved around relationships. That's the way deals were made and revenue was ultimately generated. When Gilliard was in HR for Disney's videogame business, he was judged by "making sure I had strong relationships across the organization. I had to talk strategy with the creative guys and business with the operations guys." But an ability to develop strong relationships determined success.

Mattel was a company where many long-term employees stayed in place and avoided taking risks. Since Mattel's culture was often resistant to change, status quo maintainers rose more than innovative thinkers. Then a newly named CEO noted that sales were flat, started to shake up the company, and sought innovative thinkers. As a corporate employee at Mattel, you had to read the corporate tea leaves to see what kind of behavior would be rewarded.

Performance Drives the Politicking

While this chapter is focusing on mastering corporate politics, it's still your performance that will drive your ascent. Performance comes first, and politicking follows.

At all companies, despite their corporate culture, moving up is based on obtaining results (see chapter 5, "Strengthening Your Performance"). "You need to focus on the business and what makes the business work. You have to show results and be able to put your own stamp on the results," Gilliard says, suggesting that without becoming a self-promoting braggart you make sure you earn credit for the revenue gains.

Mastering Several Cultures at Once

When forty-six-year-old Stephanie Royster, who is an African American woman based in St. Petersburg, Florida, and now runs the Agency, a public relations and public affairs company aimed at working with governmental agencies, started as a systems analyst at Xerox Corporation in 1981, she knew from her undergraduate business courses at USC that she'd have to master corporate politics and understand the corporate culture. But she quickly learned at Xerox that she'd have to master numerous cultures, not just a dominant one. "There's a department culture, a culture with your boss, and a culture with your co-workers," she says. All of the cultures were interrelated, and she had to learn what worked in each of them in order to advance.

When Royster arrived at Xerox, she thought the playing field would be level, and her intellect and professionalism would help her rise to her maximum potential. "The reality was that despite your ability, if you were not playing politics correctly, you would be derailed," she explains. She learned quickly that if she was going to advance, she had to learn the rules of corporate politics and learn to play it well, and that superior performance alone would not determine advancement. To move up, she concentrated on "winning friends and influencing people."

One of her first lessons in mastering corporate culture dealt with her boss. Starting at Xerox, the articulate and outspoken Royster knew more about business trends and strategy than her boss did. When her boss gave her a plan to execute, Royster immediately saw its flaws. But she learned quickly that her boss was easily threatened and defensive, and if she came on too strong and attacked the plan, she would alienate her boss. Instead, she asked politely if trying another way to execute the plan was feasible. Royster asked the question in such a way that the boss would not get defensive and could easily say, "If you find a better way, do it, but check with me." Avoiding alienating your boss was one early lesson that she learned at Xerox.

Swallow Your Pride

After Royster left Xerox and eventually became a vice president in Collaborative Development at the American Cancer Society (ACS) in Tampa, Florida, she participated at a meeting where she suggested that ACS collaborate with the American Heart Association and the American Diabetes Association and create one unified message for African Americans and other minorities to steer them away from unhealthy practices. Royster felt that minorities were inundated by divergent messages that got diluted. That idea was rejected. Soon after, the ACS adopted this practice when someone else higher up suggested it. Royster attributed the rejection of her idea to the fact that she was an African American woman and so sometimes her suggestions were discounted. In her own small way, she built collaborations with other medical associations at health fairs to implement her ideas. She learned that stewing about being overlooked would get her nowhere, and instead made the best of a difficult situation.

She also learned that African American women who come on too strong are branded as "the angry black woman," which is equivalent to writing your ticket out of the company. She learned to use "charm and candor" to get ahead. She managed to be assertive but tone down any indications of anger, even when her innovative ideas were shelved until someone else suggested them.

Learn Who Supports You and Who Doesn't

When Royster worked at IBM in the mid-1980s, she reported to a manager who was an African American woman. Because Royster was outgoing, bright, and quick to offer her point of view, her manager was threatened by her. Eventually that relationship turned sour and was the most instrumental reason that Royster left IBM. "I found my least support came from African American women," says Royster. "I found my greatest support for advancing came from white men," who weren't threatened by her outspokenness.

Advancing in Nonprofit Organizations

Having worked at IBM, Xerox, Peat Marwick, the ACS, the White House, and the Department of Housing and Urban Development, Royster has operated in profit-making and nonprofit cultures. In her view, advancing in nonprofits is "a less daunting process because their orientation is more conducive to minority employment." Because most nonprofits, like the ACS, address minority needs and consider minorities among their core constituencies, nonprofits hire minority employees in large numbers and, while obstacles exist, will promote them. At the ACS, Royster started in Corporate Development and became a vice president of Collaborative Initiatives.

Though nonprofits don't have the same revenue goals as IBM or Xerox, money can still play a role. When Royster organized an event at the ACS, if it raised $200,000 and appealed to 3,700 of its core members, it could be deemed a success. "Money can be a measuring stick," she says.

Balance Being Inner- and Outer-Directed

Sociologist David Riesman's influential book *The Lonely Crowd* noted that inner-directed people are self-reliant and worry little what others are thinking, while outer-directed people base much of what they do on what others think of them. Amy Titus suggests that minority employees moving up the ladder have to be a combination of both inner- and outer-directed. The further you advance, the lonelier it gets. First of all, there are fewer and fewer minority senior managers at most companies. Hence, you have to rely on yourself, be comfortable in your own skin, and not get bent out of shape by others' disapproval. On the other hand, you must always be responsive to other people, employ tact and diplomacy to be effective, delegate to staff, and operate as a team player. You've got to walk the tightrope between being immune to what others say in some ways, and responsive to everyone in other ways.

Get Your Companies to Play a More Active Role

A very talented and progressive HR person in technology at a major financial-services company in New York complains that the company can't hold on to its talented upper-level minorities. They either burn out and leave the company, are recruited by another company, or move on to entrepreneurial endeavors. But what exactly is the company doing to retain them? Many minority employees don't have the right skill set to master corporate politics and need some assistance from the company. If training is offered in sales or human resources, why can't there be training about corporate politics?

Some, but not all, companies have mentoring programs. Most have affinity groups that encourage networking. But most of the programs appeal to people at the lower rungs. As you move up the corporate ladder, you're increasingly on your own. Why not encourage your company to launch a high-level mentoring or networking program? Why not have senior vice presidents and CFOs and COOs teach talented minorities about the art of mastering corporate politics? Companies need to go the extra mile to retain their talented staff.

Action Steps

- Contact your informal networks to learn more about their view of what your company is looking for in senior executives. Are they promoting based on generating bottom-line results, becoming a team player, managing upward, impressing higher-ups, or all of the above?

- Identify the senior executives in your department who will determine promotions. Try to network with them, join task forces with them, and find opportunities to showcase your talents.

- Always manage up. Determine what your boss's expectations are of your work, and your boss's boss's expectations. Deliver the goods.

- Build your case for promotion. Strengthen your performance, build results, make as many connections as possible, and make sure you know exactly the criteria for advancement in your division. What role do colleagues play? Customers?

- Obtain the plum assignments. Find out which areas your company is basing its future development on. If you're at GE, that could well be future sales in China, India, and other Third World countries. Become an expert on growth revenue in these areas.

- Find your own voice in corporate circles. Royster learned to be assertive but not to come across as angry, which would alienate people.

- Maintain positive relationships with everyone, including secretaries, administrative assistants, sales staff, and operations people. Everyone in the company can become your supporter and burnish your reputation.

- Strive to make your boss look good. Understand how he or she is being judged. Deliver results.

- Read the corporate tea leaves. Six Sigma can be in vogue today and passé tomorrow. ISO 9000 is topical today but will be placed on the back burner tomorrow. China was nowhere in 1990, and is a growth country in 2006.

- We read Shakespeare today because he understood character and people's motivations. So must you. Understanding the CEO's and CFO's character can be influential in determining what your company seeks in senior managers, since they set the tone.

- Find commonalities with senior managers. If you both collect coins or send your children to a local public school or read Malcolm Gladwell's books, it can serve as a connection between you and them.

- Learn to be tactful and diplomatic. If you blurt out what you think at meetings and offend other senior managers, your reputation as a rebel or for bluntness can impair your ability to move up.

- Strategize, strategize, strategize. Every move you make can set you up for the future. Joining a task force on your company's future sales can position you as an expert in growth trends, which can get you promoted.

5

STRENGTHENING YOUR PERFORMANCE

T EN YEARS AGO, minority employees thought that they could not be touched by the onslaught of downsizing. Affirmative action was the buzzword of the day, and companies strove to hire talented minority professionals. Because companies were so intent on improving their diversity numbers and hiring more African Americans, Latinos, Asians, and women, minority employees thought they were protected and would be saved from the ills of downsizing, and even, at times, lackluster performance. Whether or not that was ever true is debatable, but the days of affirmative action saving jobs of minority employees are over.

By 2006, the playing field has become more level (though majority people still enter most companies with inherent advantages) when it comes to performance. Performance is key, and rising up the corporate ladder depends on results. In most cases, results boil down to efforts that affect the company's financial performance, helping the company boost its revenue, expand its market share, and enhance its products.

One candidate I recently interviewed told me about something that happened during her performance appraisal. "I don't care if you're black or a woman," her manager said. "What are your numbers?" Making your financial projections is critical to establishing superior performance. As another minority candidate noted, exceeding your goals, not just attaining them, is expected. Whether you were born in Biloxi or Jakarta is immaterial, but making the numbers determines success.

Of course, minorities often have to exceed the performance of their colleagues. In order to compete, you need to stay one step ahead of the competition. If you're in HR, you need to develop a new strategy to retain talented employees, not just continue the status quo. If you're in marketing, create a new approach to expand your customer base. Focus on knowing exactly what is expected of you and then create a game plan for exceeding expectations at every skill and task.

Not only must your performance be first rate, but also you must let senior managers know that you are responsible for generating the results, including expanding market share, increasing revenue, or developing a new outreach strategy. As stated in previous chapters, influencing decision makers and learning to toot your own horn are as important as garnering results. If you do good work and nobody notices, you'll be ignored and passed over for a promotion. Getting credit and recognition is your responsibility; don't expect senior managers to tap you on the shoulder and notice your efforts unless you call attention to them.

Though companies talk about work/life balance, becoming an industry superstar often entails working more than a typical eight-hour day. Becoming a fast-track performer involves doing all the extras that make you an outstanding performer, including joining task forces, volunteering for extra assignments, networking effectively, attending workshops and meetings, and staying visible to senior management and responsive to your peers. On the one hand, your performance will drive your success. On the other hand, you need to make sure that senior executives recognize that you are an outstanding contributor.

Strengthening your performance also entails making sure you have every possible tool in your career tool kit. If you're missing one tool or forget to impress your boss's boss, it may lead to your downfall. If you're an outstanding performer but don't network, you'll fall behind your majority colleagues. Underpinning all of your efforts is your performance. Concentrate on exceeding your job description, and then you can venture off into exploring new challenges. Since forging strong relationships and managing upward are critical to advancing, you'll need to make sure you pay as much attention to developing those connections as you do to completing your normal job tasks. You have to use all of the tools in your kit to advance, not settle for one or two.

Benchmark your performance against your colleagues'; it's another way to strengthen performance. What are your colleagues doing? What can you do to outshine and outperform them? What new area or skill can you adopt that will differentiate you as a performer? What new strategy can you introduce to boost revenue? What did your predecessor do, and what can you do better? What missteps have others taken that you can avoid? Take a step back and evaluate your performance objectively. Determine what you can do better.

And yet, despite all of the emphasis on becoming a superior performer, competency determines only one portion of attaining success in corporate America. Majority employees can usually advance with competent performance, but more is expected of minorities. Because many senior majority managers have lingering doubts about the competence of minority employees, minorities often have to be superior performers, work harder and smarter, and go the extra mile in order to be considered managerial and senior-level material.

Hence, minority employees have to transcend competence and become superstars. Corporations expect that accountants know debits and assets and IT professionals know about software and spreadsheets, so technical know-how is a baseline skill. Much of success depends on chemistry between the employee and the corporation, being in the forefront of seeking out leadership opportunities and making a name for yourself, developing a cultural fit between you and the company, building relationships at the company, and understanding the minefields that undermine your efforts. As Paulette Mullings suggested in the previous chapter, senior managers won't spell out exactly what it takes to succeed or gain promotion. You have to use your critical-thinking skills to read between the lines and figure out what the clues are that lead to promotion.

In order to be considered ripe for advancement, you have to be relentless. Like a tennis pro who practices seven days a week and eight hours a day to become ranked number one, you have to pursue excellence unrelentingly. And many minority candidates face hushed doubts behind their back, even belittling slights and overt racism, so you'll have to possess thick skin, totally believe in yourself, and never lose sight of your target: helping the company achieve its goals, being true to yourself, and advancing your own career.

Mistake #1: Playing the Race/Gender Card

Too many minority candidates use race or gender as an excuse for poor performance. My division generated only $1 million, and my majority counterpart produced $2 million in revenue, but he had all the advantages including the better area and more experienced people. Excuses won't do anymore. On a level playing field, you have to find a way to outperform all of your colleagues. By thinking strategically you'll find new ways to win, generate more revenue, and find new ways to extend your market share.

Turn the race card upside down to succeed. Because you're an outsider working for a mainstream company, you'll be able to think of new ways to generate revenue that the status quo seekers overlook.

Mistake #2: Not Leveraging Your Internal Resources

The entire corporation and its internal staff offer resources that you have to tap. If you close off communication, you cut yourself off from unearthing new information that will strengthen your performance. You have to search constantly for new information. What is your boss seeking? What new information is your boss's boss seeking? What's the new initiative that is driving your company's profit growth? You need to be asking questions, contacting your informal and formal networks, and tapping all resources to stay one step ahead of all colleagues.

Mistake #3: Lapsing into Complacency

Moving up the corporate ladder involves a relentless pursuit of success. Becoming a vice president is only a launching pad. I've seen too many candidates who are promoted to vice president and then sit back and think they have it made. Promotions will come one after another, and all they have to do is go along for the ride, many think. In fact, the opposite is true. Complacency leads to poor performance and getting stuck. Being named a vice president enables you to set your sights higher and aim to become a managing director or senior vice president. It will require self-initiative, outthinking your colleagues, and superior performance to keep moving up the ladder. You have to challenge yourself constantly, learn new skills, keep abreast of changing trends, and appeal to an ever-expanding audience, and not fall victim to complacency.

Mistake #4: Not Keeping Pace with Your Majority Colleagues

Meeting the sales goals of your manager won't be enough to get promoted. You'll have to exceed what's expected of a majority colleague, not match it. Hence, you have to stay one step ahead of your majority colleagues by introducing new sales strategies, devising new techniques, and outsmarting them. The corporation tells you that everyone is equal and everyone has the opportunity to rise to his or her natural level of success. The reality is that you lack the connections of the old boys' network, and you'll have to outperform your majority colleagues to advance.

Mistake #5: Ignoring the Power Circles

The Lone Ranger was a Western hero who fought and overcame bad guys, assisted by Tonto, his American Indian sidekick. A Lone Ranger, however, doesn't succeed in corporate America. Hence, minority employees have to gain acceptance into the power corridors of America. Successful minority CEOs such as Ken Chenault, Stan O'Neal, Solomon Trujillo, Andrea Jung, Fred Thompson, Carlos Gutierrez, and Richard Parsons gained the influence and trust of the

top senior executives of their company. They were not solo performers, but team players who knew something about corporate politics,
securing a godfather, and obtaining results.

Some minority candidates view gaining favor from senior managers as selling out. I view building relationships with senior executives as understanding the corporate landscape, developing strong
relationships with power brokers, and using your communication
skills at their highest level.

Overcoming the Unwritten Code

Majority senior executives would never disclose this to you, but the
truth of the matter is many expect that talented minorities, even the
ones with MBAs from Harvard, Wharton, or Columbia, will not be
as bright as white MBAs from the same school. No matter what they
say, and no matter how they try to obscure their true thoughts, they
think that African Americans, Latinos, Asians, and women won't
perform as well. They believe that minorities and women may have
the technical skills but lack the street-smarts, toughness, and ability
to make difficult decisions, or possess the requisite experience to
wield influence at the upper echelon. That's partially why many minorities advance to vice president and then are prevented from gaining promotions beyond that.

Overcoming that low expectation requires mastering all the
skills that I am describing. Talented minority employees have to be
one step ahead of their majority colleagues in order to dispel the notion that they are not good enough. The reality is they are good
enough and in fact, often, are smarter, but the majority senior executives will distort any one mistake or failure out of proportion to support their thesis that the African American MBA from Wharton got

his or her degree only because of affirmative action. Even when the courts have taken the teeth out of affirmative action, majority executives cling to the belief that minorities don't have the skills or intelligence to advance to the senior executive corridor. Disproving that should serve as enough motivation to keep you pumped up to excel at every possible opportunity.

It's More Than Mastering Skills

Having been raised in a family where no one had ever worked in a corporation, many minority employees start their careers with a goal of becoming the best accountant, logistics planner, or corporate communications director. But that won't be sufficient. You have to go beyond your job description. Moving up requires going beyond your business area, becoming an expert in a certain area, speaking at conferences, and making a name for yourself.

Just as in college, where you need to get an A or B+ average to get into the top-tier schools and also participate in extracurricular activities to differentiate you from other students, the same is true in corporate life. You must master all the technical skills of your job. But then you must constantly think about going beyond your job description. What external organizations can you join where you can appear on panels and invite senior executives to hear you speak? That's one way to make a name for yourself. Volunteering at nonprofit organizations serves as another way to showcase your talent, test your presentation skills, meet senior executives at your company as well as others who are also volunteering, and help out a worthy cause that motivates you. It's a true win-win.

The accountants who want to be superior performers can concentrate on mastering financials and becoming skilled at their job. But in my view, becoming competent is like juggling only one ball in the air. Minority employees who want to advance have to become skilled at keeping several balls in the air: the networking ball, the mentoring ball, the volunteering ball, the building-relationships-with-senior-managers ball, the self-initiating-to-join-task-force ball, etc.

Constantly Assess the Landscape

I placed a minority senior executive at one of the country's largest homebuilders. He was hired by the company's HR director, who was considered a visionary at developing minorities. The HR director knew that one-quarter of the company's growth projection in the next few years stemmed from selling homes to the growing Latino, African American, and Asian market. To expand the company's market and reach minorities, he hired talented people of color from other companies who could help this homebuilder in its growth projections. In 2005, this HR chief resigned from the company, and the commitment to diversity left with him.

The newly hired senior executive called and told me that "inclusion" was no longer the buzzword at the company, and he had to prove himself all over again as a top performer. He knew that he would have to make adjustments in his performance to maintain his fast-track status, since one of the company's main diversity champions had departed. Because he was able to constantly read the corporate tea leaves and adjust to a changing culture, he maintained his position and influence and was still poised to advance.

Contrast that with another candidate who joined a company that for years had been a steady but stodgy place to work. But the new CEO decided to overhaul the company's vision and business, stretched its revenue projections, and demanded new and innovative strategic thinking. Status quo was out; creative thinking was in. But this candidate didn't make any adjustments. Ignoring the cultural shifts, he proceeded along his merry way, operating the same as he had when the company was in a steady state. Despite earning a high salary and being recruited by the company from a Fortune 500 powerhouse, he was dismissed after a year. He didn't read the corporate tea leaves and adjust to a changing environment, and consequently lost his job.

Succumbing to Faulty Perceptions

More than majority corporate employees, minority employees fall victim to a distorted sense of their own performance. Part of why this happens stems from the performance-appraisal system, where managers are often trained to withhold honest feedback from minorities, offer bland descriptions of performance, and often rate a minority employee higher than they really believe. One majority executive told me that his financial-services company was so wary of minority employees suing the company (because it had had more than its share of legal suits settled for six figures out of court) that managers were told to whitewash (no pun intended) their performance appraisals so that minority employees would have no ammunition for a future case. Hence, it's imperative that minority employees use their informal and formal networks and mentors to learn what their real standing is in the division and company. Are you on the fast track? What do you have to do to move up? What new skills must you add?

Deciphering the Code

In order to play the game at the highest level, rise to the level of vice president, and keep advancing, you have to master another unwritten code of corporate America. Senior executives won't spell out exactly what it takes to advance. You'll have to question, elicit direction, and lean on your mentors and informal networks to gauge what it will take at your company to advance (without appearing to be too aggressive or making your job pursuit more important than your job). It's up to you to learn to publicize your own efforts without antagonizing anyone or coming across as self-serving, to reach out to senior executives in your division and ascertain what their expectations are, to master the art of tact and diplomacy so you don't alienate anyone, and to build bridges in the corporation because you never know who can help you advance. That requires operating all the time on all six cylinders and never being satisfied with a halfhearted effort. Your antennae have to be out at all times, discerning changes in leadership and alterations in the company's direction, and then you must fit into that changing landscape.

It All Starts with Your Manager—Climbing the Ladder

Monica Pool Ross, who is forty years old and a director for human resources at Sony Corporation's office in San Diego, started her corporate career fifteen years ago as a supervisor in HR at GTE and worked her way up the corporate ladder to HR manager at PepsiCo before joining Sony. Because of the many obstacles that minorities face advancing, everything "starts with a manager," she says. "You have to make sure your manager has some key attributes that will enable you to operate at your maximum potential." Ross describes the ideal manager who can help a minority employee develop as possessing these characteristics: sets high performance expectations; seeks growth opportunities for her staff; shares credit with her staff; challenges her employees to perform better and provides constant feedback; encourages different points of view; and avoids being dogmatic.

If your manager has minimal ambition and drive and focuses only on the status quo and getting by, you probably won't learn new skills and will be thwarted in your ability to move up. If your manager is ethically challenged and is breaking rules and tries to compromise your integrity, it can also damage your career and reputation, Ross says. "You'll be affected by guilt by association." So once you select an area to work in, making sure your manager is a top-flight performer who can train you will help launch your career.

For example, when Ross, whose heritage is Seminole Indian, French, Irish, and African American, was first starting out, she worked for an African American manager who arrived forty-five minutes late nearly every day, and always had an excuse for her tardiness. She consistently missed deadlines, but always managed to leave the office the minute the clock struck 5 p.m. She managed to befriend many of her African American staff, but failed to stay in touch with senior executives who were directing her department. When Ross told her that her department was falling behind in its responsibilities, the manager defended her performance. Finally, that manager was transferred out of the department. Ross's point here is that when an ethnic employee works for a minority manager, different problems can arise.

Ross advises doing your homework about your prospective manager. Ask people you know in the company about how she treats her staff, whether the manager is open to minorities, and whether other staff members have moved up under that manager's tutelage. "Make sure it's the right manager and the right role for you. Don't get sidetracked by money alone," she adds.

Understanding Expectations

Once you and your manager have established a strong, positive relationship, then you can develop your skills, critical for strengthening your performance and setting yourself up for success. But since managers are often understated and laconic giving performance appraisals to their staff, and especially their minority staff, it is imperative that you ask for feedback, Ross suggests. Some managers are quite skillful at providing feedback, and the feedback will happen naturally. But most aren't. "Ask for frequent feedback," she advises. Make sure you know exactly what is expected of you, what your evaluation is being based on, and what your bonus, if applicable, will be judged on. Don't try to read between the lines of your manager's expectations; ensure that everything is explicitly stated. The onus, Ross stresses, is on you to make sure you know the expectations; don't sit back and fault the manager for not providing them.

Adjust to the Manager

When Ross was an HR manager at GTE, a junior employee came into her office to complain about her new manager. "My manager doesn't understand the way it works here," she told Ross. Her new manager was changing the way the department ran and was altering expectations of employees. Ross sat the employee down and explained that when a new manager is named, it's the employee who must adjust to the manager, not vice versa. Being flexible, adjusting to the new demands, and making alterations are critical to strengthening performance at a company that is constantly changing.

Focus on Bottom-Line Results

Though Sony Corporation, PepsiCo, and GTE/Verizon were in very different industries, in terms of performance expected from employee, they had one thing in common: you needed to understand how your job affected the bottom line. Ross, the HR manager-director, had direct influence over profit and revenue by recruiting, hiring, and developing talent. She could also focus on reducing costs in her area as well as contributing to increasing revenue. If she served on a cross-functional team, she would devise strategies that could increase sales or improve marketing, even though she was in HR. In order to strengthen performance, you "must understand exactly how your role can influence the bottom line," she says.

Too Much Politicking Can Be Harmful

As demonstrated in the previous chapter, mastering corporate politics is essential to advancing. But Ross has seen a number of minority candidates who were so ambitious that excessive politicking led to their downfall. She recalls one junior executive who spent a considerable amount of time arranging one-on-one background meetings with senior managers. At those meetings, he'd ask each of them what was the best route for him to take to get a promotion. Since many of these managers were in touch with one another, they started to perceive him as an overly aggressive go-getter. But most important, he stopped paying attention to performing his actual job and executing it well. Hence, his performance suffered. He was so intent on moving up that he became a subpar performer who thought that his aggressiveness and drive would be enough to advance. His inadequate performance led to his being fired.

Overcoming Gender Stereotypes

Everyone in a corporation has a distinct reputation. You're the hard worker, the opinionated one, the shy one, the one who asks questions. But Ross says that female employees in general, and especially women minority employees, face tremendous hurdles in establishing a communication style that is honest and yet doesn't offend others. When Ross was starting out at GTE, she attended a meeting, asked some questions that seemed harmless and straightforward to her, and was told by her manager that she was coming across as overly aggressive. If a man had asked those questions, she suggests, it would have been acceptable, but women can easily threaten people. Yet Ross is very outgoing and has strong convictions, and she didn't want to squelch her ability to ask questions. She has since learned to frame her questions tactfully, speak diplomatically, but still ask questions when appropriate. She wants to come across as assertive but not accusatory or overly aggressive.

Surmounting the Obstacles

Despite all the obstacles that Ross faced in her career, she has been promoted several times and is now a director of human resources at Sony. Minority employees "have an opportunity to succeed in corporate America. We are the drivers of our destiny. Are there obstacles? Indeed," she says, answering her own question. But she adds that many majority people also face obstacles because they were raised in rural America, were born working-class, had parents who didn't attend college, had alcoholism in the family, etc. Success stems from believing in yourself; then you must build strong relationships at the company, develop support groups in the company, constantly obtain feedback, and always focus on your job performance, Ross says.

Managing the Inattentive Majority Manager

Though Ross has built many strong relationships with majority executives in her various companies and has been supported by many majority senior vice presidents, she has also observed many majority executives who don't understand the obstacles that minority employees face. "They think that everyone operates on a level playing field," she says. "They don't understand the world in which we operate" and the challenges that minority women and men face adjusting to a predominantly majority corporation. "If you brought majority males and placed them in an all-black environment, they might be uncomfortable," she says. But majority executives don't consider that minorities face subtle slights, belittling views, and lower expectations than majority employees.

So, Ross says, minorities have to "obtain opportunities to show their talents and shine, excel at what they do, make sure they're building bridges to others, work as a team, and work like hell." Ross took seriously her mom's adage that minorities "have to work twice as hard to receive half the credit."

Tackle the Tough Assignments

Ross has seen innumerable minority staff do a competent job. But when it comes to accepting high-risk assignments, they often shy away from tackling them. "When the team is down by one point with six seconds left on the clock, Michael Jordan wants the ball," she says. Fearful of failing and not wanting to let down their majority senior executives, minority employees often reject the high-profile assignments. Ross suggests that you make things happen and want the ball just as Jordan did. With high-risk assignments comes high reward, she adds. Volunteer to lead a cross-functional team that can catapult your business into new revenue areas. Define your job by what you think you can accomplish, not just what your job description says.

Aligning Yourself with the Company's Goals

When Tony Brown, who is director of staffing at Bear Stearns, a financial-services company in New York, enters a room, he makes a strong impression. He's an imposing six-foot-five-inch African American who comes across as self-assured and confident. He's so confident that he doesn't have to call attention to his strong academic credentials, which include a bachelor's degree from Harvard University and an MBA from Stanford Business School. Brown's climb up the corporate ladder includes stints as a managing director and partner at Gilbert Tweed, an executive search firm; engagement manager at well-respected McKinsey & Company; managing director of the Management Consulting Group at Bankers Trust Company; principal at Egon Zehnder International, an executive search firm; and vice president of International Money Markets at Lehman Brothers.

What's enabled Brown to advance is his ability to, in his words, "align himself with what the company is trying to get done." When he joins a company, he strives to understand what the company is trying to achieve and what he can do to help the company meet its goals. Because he's worked in different industries, one of the first things he's done when joining a company is to seek out experienced people, and learn from them by asking about the company's goals and direction.

For example, in one of Brown's first stints, as a manufacturing analyst at COBE Laboratories, a producer of high-tech medical products, his boss was given a mandate to reduce inventory for electromagnetism, which is involved in the making of dialysis machines, by $500,000. Realizing that this was a high priority, which was being audited on a regular basis, Brown set out to reduce his area's inventory. Eventually, he reduced inventory in his business unit by $500,000. He was able to meet his division's goal by himself, without requiring any additional reduction from the five or six other managers. His reward was a promotion. "As I looked around, I noticed that the people who were fastest moving were the ones less focused on advancing and more focused on getting the job done," he says.

Sometimes aligning with the company's goal isn't always about dollars and cents. When he worked as a consultant at McKinsey & Company and was working on a project at Lehman Brothers's Institutional Fixed Income Trading Department, his manager wanted to develop a strong relationship with the senior manager in charge of that department. But that Lehman Brothers manager was so busy that he didn't make the time to schedule an interview.

Seizing the opportunity, Brown, who had previously worked at Lehman Brothers and had a positive relationship with the manager, sought him out and asked him if he would make time to meet with his McKinsey manager. He did, which led to McKinsey's forming a stronger relationship with Lehman, which happened because of Brown's efforts.

Brown focused on his ability to read the corporate tea leaves and figure out each business's priorities and overarching goals. Developing strong relationships and a strong internal network was critical to his unearthing this information. He recommends that you develop close relationships with your boss, your boss's boss, and other influential decision makers at your firm. At Bear Stearns, he says, "not much is written down in manuals. If you don't develop a set of colleagues and mentors that can give you direction, it will take you a long time to figure out how to get it done."

Avoiding Complacency

One of the traps that Brown sees minorities fall into more often than majority candidates is "nesting." By "nesting," he means getting too comfortable, avoiding taking risks, and finding yourself stuck in your current job, with little chance of advancement. As a former executive recruiter with Egon Zehnder International, he contacted many minority and majority candidates about pursuing options that could further their career. Often, he found women and minorities more reluctant to make a change than majority candidates. Since minority candidates often had to prove themselves in their current job, overcome many obstacles, and convince the naysayers and critics, many didn't want to face the anxiety of starting over again. Many stayed put, satisfied with their current salary and work conditions, and unwilling to take the plunge into a new scenario, which could advance their career.

Unlike many minorities, Brown challenged himself and took

risks, changing jobs, moving into new industries, moving up the ranks. Why was he able to take risks when many minorities avoided them? He attributes his ability to take risks to a variety of factors, including possessing thick skin and not being overly concerned about what others think of him and yet at the same time demonstrating an uncanny ability to quickly build rapport with a variety of people in his new firm. He can enter a firm, stay focused on the company's objectives and his role in achieving them, and make a place for himself at the new company. Having attended a private school in Riverdale, New York, he's been comfortable in integrated surroundings since he was thirteen years old.

Take Risks

When Brown was approached by Bear Stearns to become its director of staffing, it was establishing a position that hitherto didn't exist. Brown knew that accepting this position would be a risk because he would have to define the job, establish its parameters, build strong relationships with several senior managers across the company, and develop the position. He knew that he could fail at these tasks, but felt that accepting the challenge was worth the risk. If he could add value, help Bear Stearns achieve its goal, it could catapult his career yet again. Accepting the risk is part of advancing up the corporate ladder.

Going Against Conventional Wisdom

Most cognoscenti of corporate life will tell you that if you want to advance in 2006 and beyond you have to find challenges, change companies, and be open to relocating to find the best opportunities. The odds are strong that most people who stay with one company for twenty-five years stagnate. But fifty-one-year-old African American Al Zollar, who since July 2004 has been general manager of Tivoli Software (a nearly $2 billion business that is part of the IBM Software Group and located in Somers, New York), started in IBM in 1977 as a systems engineer trainee and has never left the company. Currently, he manages more than four thousand people in his division, attesting to how he has climbed the corporate ladder without having to leave IBM.

Because IBM is such a complex company, Zollar has faced numerous internal moves and challenges. He has been a manager of IBM Software Development Labs, lab director for the IBM Software Group in Raleigh, North Carolina, and general manager of IBM's Networking Computing Software Division. Each new role helped him build his technical skills, expand his repertoire, and in most cases, climb the ladder. "In order for me to gain this experience in the IT industry, I would have had to work at five or six different companies. Because of the unique range of experiences at IBM, I could stay within the same company," he says.

Focus on Your Technical Skills

Zollar admits that when he joined IBM in 1977, "I was very naïve about business. When I started at IBM, I wouldn't know about corporate politics if it hit me in the face." In fact, his first day on the job he wore bell-bottom pants, platform shoes, and a seersucker suit, and had a goatee—not exactly the IBM image. Gradually he learned to adapt to the IBM culture and wear three-piece pin-striped suits, wingtip shoes, and white shirts.

Despite his naïveté, Zollar knew exactly what he wanted to accomplish when he started at IBM: he focused on delivering superior performance. "As a systems engineer, it's your technical skills that separate you from others," he says. To achieve that goal, Zollar absorbed as much information as he could about IBM's products and codes, studied the software, and often stayed late poring over manuals on his own time. His goal was to be the best-prepared systems engineer so that he could impress IBM's customers and deliver outstanding performance. Furthermore, he says that at entry-level jobs, the politics is not as thick as in senior management, so performance is the driving force.

Having impressed senior managers during the IBM training, Zollar was selected for IBM's early identification program, which was really a management-training program. He participated in a special training program and received management training. He was assigned to handle the San Francisco account of I Magnin, a now defunct chain of high-end women's department stores.

Make Your Manager an Ally

Working on the I Magnin account, Zollar encountered his first major crisis at IBM. One of the main data center managers at I Magnin that he collaborated with hailed from Mississippi and did not want to work with an African American IBM employee. He contacted Zollar's boss and informed the manager that he wanted Zollar removed from his position.

But Zollar had impressed his manager with his work ethic and technical expertise, and she believed in his skills and potential. Defending him, she told the I Magnin data center manager that Zollar was one of the three most knowledgeable systems engineers that she had ever worked with at IBM and that she was leaving him in the position for ninety days. At the end of that time period, if he wasn't happy with Zollar's performance, it would consider making a switch.

Performance Must Wow and Impress

Bright and enterprising, and viewing himself as a problem solver, Zollar set out to fix the problems of that data center. He worked ten to twelve hours a day and prepared a set of recommendations to improve the data center's operation. Working nights and weekends, he navigated the project through a variety of critical rough spots and finally turned that data center around. The data center's problems were fixed and started to run smoothly. At the end of ninety days, when his manager asked her I Magnin counterpart what he thought, he replied, "Please don't take Zollar off the account. He's too good."

Zollar learned several important things from this early account. One was that to move up the corporate ladder, you needed to find a sponsor. He differentiates between mentoring, which is more about counseling and coaching, and sponsorship, which involves gaining the confidence of your manager and his or her boss. "You want management to say 'Al Zollar can do this job. I'll put my reputation on the line.' When a boss believes you can do the job, that can establish your reputation," he says. That sponsorship revolves around your providing excellent, reliable, and superior performance.

Having gained the confidence and sponsorship of his manager, Zollar was able to obtain more challenging projects. For example, when he was still a systems engineer, IBM was facing a problem with a client, Bank of America, because a software defect was causing its automated teller machines to malfunction. Bank of America's customer service was affected, as was its reputation, since it triggered a news story in a daily newspaper in San Francisco, where the bank was headquartered. After three days, IBM still hadn't found the root cause of the problem.

Zollar volunteered for the assignment and worked collaboratively with a team. "We worked around the clock, often not getting any sleep. But we found the problem and fixed it," he says. Based on Zollar's contribution and on his involvement in solving a software problem, he was promoted. The moral here, he says, is "You have to put yourself on the line." These were difficult situations, and he admits that failure was a possibility in both cases. But because Zollar solved these problems, senior managers took notice and rewarded him.

Consider Lateral Moves

Most readers of this book want to move up the corporate ladder and ascend quickly in order to achieve the goals in their strategic career blueprint. But Zollar's ascent proves that moving up the corporate ladder doesn't always involve a direct climb; sometimes lateral moves can play an essential role.

When Zollar accepted the role of lab director at the IBM Software Group in Raleigh, North Carolina, many at IBM questioned that move. Why make a lateral move at the same salary? they wondered. But Zollar was looking at his long-term strategic plan, not for immediate gratification or earning a couple of thousand dollars more a year. By accepting this position, he was expanding his portfolio of skills. He was managing multiple products instead of one product, strengthening his skills, expanding his résumé, and positioning himself for senior management positions in the future. In fact, when he was named general manager of Tivoli Software, some of his competitors had managed only one product, and his broadened skills may have given him the edge.

Though Zollar is now politically astute, he still claims that it was his performance, more than gamesmanship, that contributed to his being named head of a four-thousand-person software division. He's learned to work cooperatively with people, listen to his supervisor and staff, communicate effectively, find commonalities among different constituencies, motivate people, and be firm when he has to.

Overcoming Personal Obstacles and Becoming Resilient

Though Zollar has become an IBM success story, when he first started on the job, he almost didn't make it through the first week. Three days after he started, his mother died unexpectedly. Since he was the oldest sibling, he had several responsibilities to take care of and was grief stricken. Coming to work was too much for him, and he offered to resign. Since IBM was an employee-centered company, his manager told him to take some time off, do what he had to do, and return to work after he tended to issues at home.

When Zollar was thirteen years old, his father was shot to death. His mother had to take several jobs and relocate the family. What did all of these personal hardships teach Zollar? "I learned to be resilient," he says. He learned to be strong in times of adversity and learned to bounce back from tough times, skills that are helpful in a corporate setting as well. "Resilience is an asset at any corporation," he says. But his best advice is "Focus on performance. The number one way to move ahead starts with your performance."

Moving from One Company to Another Can Pay Off

Contrary to Al Zollar, who has stayed at IBM for twenty-eight years, Kirk Forrest, who is a fifty-four-year-old African American with a law degree from Harvard Law School, moved up the corporate ladder at several companies before being named a general counsel. He is currently general counsel at New York–based Minerals Technologies, a leading supplier of minerals serving industrial markets. Previously he served as associate general counsel at the William Companies after it acquired Mapco (where he worked as general counsel), general counsel at Sam's Club, senior counsel at International Paper, and counsel at Xerox. For Forrest, taking risks and relocating to Stamford, Connecticut, for Xerox; San Francisco as partner in Carroll, Burdick & McDonough; and Tulsa, Oklahoma, for Mapco has paid off.

Performance Is Measurable

Though some experts say that all performance evaluation is ultimately subjective, no matter what the criteria, Forrest says that performance, even for an attorney and general counsel, is measurable. He acknowledges that a general counsel "doesn't make widgets. It's hard to show the bottom-line result from a counsel." But he insists that "you can measure the quality of the advice, results it achieved, and cost saving in any negotiation."

Having worked at several Fortune 500 companies as a general counsel and as a partner at a law firm, he has learned to adapt to a variety of corporate and legal cultures. He strives to pinpoint how each culture operates. Forrest says that in some cultures the top brass makes decisions on its own and doesn't want anyone else's involvement. That kind of culture means he won't even try to get involved in decision making. But if the culture is inclusive and senior managers are receptive to input, he'll offer suggestions. Knowing the culture is key to your performance.

Dealing with Expectations

Many minority executives say that minorities face pressures that majority candidates don't. Even Forrest, who stresses that performance is measurable and that performance determines success, admits that ambitious minorities "have to double-check what they do to make certain it's right. Majority people might be given an extra chance, but if you're a minority female and flub the first assignment, you don't get a second." Hence, Forrest has learned that he must fully prepare for any assignment, always strive to perform the most intensive research, and always anticipate what his clients will ask of him.

What have been the most significant reasons why Forrest has become chief counsel of a leading private firm in its industry? Performance, performance, performance, he replies. He always focuses on producing superior results. He accepts challenges, takes risks, and has shown that he can conquer any challenge. When he started as general counsel at Sam's Club, he knew little about retail, but asked the right questions, found a mentor, and in a short time became knowledgeable. "Ultimately, moving up is about performance," he says.

Action Steps

- Conduct extensive due diligence on the expectations at your job. Find out what specifically is expected of you. In your first year on the job, dedicate yourself to excelling. Al Zollar stayed late numerous nights to read manuals and understand the products and become technically proficient in his job. That laid the groundwork for his subsequent success.

- Your performance will establish your reputation. You will become Al Zollar the problem solver, Tony Brown who delivers results, Monica Pool Ross who understands the culture. If you're late ever day or delinquent with assignments, you will soon become the ex-employee.

- Ask your internal network exactly what is expected of you. Sometimes managers are not forthcoming, and performance appraisals reveal only a shade of what is going on. Learn the real deal about what is expected.

- Whatever your job description is, concentrate on exceeding demands. If each area is asked to reduce inventory by $100,000, find ways to go beyond that, just as Tony Brown did at COBE Laboratories.

- Avoid making any excuses about being African American, Latino, female, Asian, or from any other ethnic group. Find ways to outdo, surmount, and exceed your majority counterparts. Tap ethnic markets to improve revenue.

- If you encounter majority senior executives who have low expectations of minorities, don't be affected by their negative outlook. Concentrate on delivering the best performance, as Kirk Forrest stressed, and everything else will fall into place.

- Adjust to the culture. Just because something was done a certain way in 2005 doesn't mean it will continue that way in 2006. Companies have very dynamic cultures and are always changing. When a new CEO or COO is named, the culture may change. Learn to become flexible and fit what you do into the overall culture.

- Obtain your cues from your manager. As Ross hinted, your manager is your most trusted ally and will have the largest influence on your career and reputation. Find out what is expected of you and deliver the goods.

- No matter what your role—even in marketing, HR, PR, or legal—you play a role in bottom-line results. You can reduce costs, improve efficiencies, join task forces to make suggestions about how to cross-sell. Make a case for how you have added value and boosted revenue or cut costs for the company.

- Focus on performance; learn about politics, but let your performance carry you up the ladder. If you only network and indulge in politicking and let your performance suffer, you'll damage your career ambitions.

- Pursue challenging assignments, and don't be afraid of failure. Zollar made a name for himself at IBM by tackling and conquering assignments that others avoided. It led to his being promoted and boosted his internal reputation.

- Align yourself with the company's goals. When Tony Brown transferred into Lehman Brothers, McKinsey, and Bear Stearns, he focused on tapping an informal network and learning exactly what the company's goals were. Then he played his role in delivering those goals.

- If you're promoted to vice president, don't sit back. That's your starting point, your launching pad. Use that to catapult your career; don't sit back and put your feet up on the chair.

- Become resilient. As minority professionals, you are going to face one hurdle after another. Climbing the corporate ladder will require a thick skin, persistence beyond belief, and a relentless pursuit of superior performance. Don't get distracted; focus on delivering superior performance and fitting into the company's culture.

6

TURNING YOUR ETHNICITY INTO
A COMPETITIVE EDGE

M ANY, BUT NOT all, minority employees start working at a corporation on the defensive. Will they fit in? Will the corporation accept them for who they are? Will they have to make adjustments to be accepted and have to hide their true personality in order to conform? Many minorities overlook the fact that they bring an array of strengths that can help the company grow, boost profits, and expand its market share by appealing to the ever growing minority audience. In addition, many minority professionals have insights and skills that reach mainstream markets.

One in eight Americans is Latino, which is the fastest-growing population in the United States. One in eight Americans is African American, and one in twenty is an Asian American. In New York, Los Angeles, Miami, and other major cities, the minority has become the majority. And that means that minority buying power is growing and proliferating. Many global companies, however, are only starting to target, reach out to, and market to minority consumers.

According to the study "The Multicultural Economy 2005," conducted by Jeffrey M. Humphreys, the director of the Selig Center for Economic Growth at the University of Georgia, the combined buying power of African Americans, Asians, and Native Americans will reach a staggering $1.7 trillion in 2010, more than triple its 1990 level of $454 billion. African Americans will account for $1 trillion of that amount. Those three minority groups will account for 14 percent of total American buying power in 2010, up from 10.6 percent in 1990. Any company that ignores marketing to the increasingly influential minority audience is hurting itself and its bottom line.

Those numbers concern race, based on U.S. Census Bureau categories, but they don't take into account ethnic groups, including the fastest-growing segment of the American population: Latinos. Latino buying power is growing exponentially, from $212 billion in 1990 to $736 billion in 2005, and is expected to reach $1 trillion in 2010, which will account for over 9 percent of American buying power. Asian buying power will increase to $579 billion in 2010 from $397 billion in 2005, and Asians will constitute nearly 5 percent of the American population in 2010 or 15 million Americans.

What do these numbers mean to a minority employee? That buying power translates into generating plenty of opportunities for minorities who can tap into new markets. The companies that understand emerging markets are the ones that will prosper in a changing marketplace. Do Hispanics buy the same kind of toothpaste as whites, or is there another way to target them? If you're in marketing at Gillette (recently acquired by Procter & Gamble), and you find a new way to tap into minority markets, you can use your expertise to help your company and help yourself move up. Is your financial-services company sensitive to the growing middle class of African Americans, Latinos, and Asians, not to mention the ever-increasing number of wealthy minority individuals? And if your company has ignored marketing to this growing audience, you might suggest ways to reach these consumers to boost revenue.

Furthermore, many minorities bring a fresh perspective that corporations crave. The mantra at many companies has been encouraging employees to "think outside the box" and operate creatively. General Electric, for example, hired "creative consultants" to inspire innovative thinking, according to a 2005 *Business Week* cover story. If you're a majority employee who is immersed in the mainstream, steeped in conformist and parochial thinking, creative thinking won't naturally emerge. But minority candidates, who grew up working-class yet gained their degree and have started moving up the ranks, bring an irreverent outsider's viewpoint that can lead to new solutions.

Minorities' adding value to a company can play out in innumerable ways, depending on whether they're working for a pharmaceutical, packaged-goods, or financial-services company. For example, pharmaceutical companies are hiring physicians of color who can help the drug companies target their products to niche and minority consumers. Physicians are also being engaged as spokespersons who can build positive community relations in minority neighborhoods. In addition, many companies employ multicultural marketers, whose job is to find ways to reach diverse audiences.

Here's the rub, however. In most cases, to move up the corporate ladder, even a skilled marketer who is raising a company's profile in and profits from African American, Asian, American Indian, or Hispanic markets must also be able to reach majority audiences. If you're good at appealing to African Americans only, you can limit your advancement. Yet many corporate employees have advanced by initially establishing their expertise at appealing to minority markets.

Corporations are realizing that targeting minority markets can generate revenue. Corona, for example, is the largest selling imported beer in the United States because it has done an effective job of reaching both Latinos and majority people. Bright, talented minority professionals can show how to develop this effective targeted marketing. Make your reputation, boost revenue, and then parlay that into a job marketing to everyone, including, but not exclusively, minorities.

Just as I have encouraged you to perform due diligence about the company, you also need to discover if your prospective company is open to hearing ideas from minorities about growing revenue and targeting emerging markets. If it's not, you might be better off considering a company that is responsive.

According to leading experts, some companies have been very aggressive about targeting minority audiences, while others have been asleep at the wheel. "Many companies get it—some have been doing multicultural marketing for years; and many don't get it and are just starting to catch up," notes Lisa Skriloff, president of Multicultural Marketing Resources, a New York–based public relations and marketing firm specializing in ethnic marketing. She recalls that in the early 1980s, Procter & Gamble, AT&T, and Bayer were targeting their products to Spanish audiences, long before the Hudson Institute in the late 1990s documented that Hispanics were the fastest-growing ethnic audience in the United States.

Skriloff sees the major obstacle to targeting niche audiences and tapping the increasing minority buying power as "getting the buy-in from top management." In her view, most companies that are located in cities such as New York, Los Angeles, and Miami, where the minority has become the majority and its influence is palpable, get it; but suburban companies that are hidden away in malls that are far away from diverse communities tend to overlook ethnic buying power. If you begin working for a company located in suburbia, away from minority strongholds, it may offer the perfect opportunity to forge a reputation and enlighten the company about targeting minority markets.

Targeted advertising to minorities has become so powerful that it can be used to reach majority audiences as well. Skriloff mentioned a Ford TV ad done by the UniWorld Group that aimed at African American buyers that was so effective that Ford decided to run it on the *Today* show and other shows. Her company publishes a directory that serves as a source book for advertising and marketing for minorities and can be downloaded for free at www.multicultural.com.

With so much emphasis on minority buying power and helping your company realize some of this market share, minority employees no longer have to see their status as an outsider but instead can view it as an asset. Still, too many minorities run scared, hide their background, and don't turn their ethnicity into a competitive edge. Here are five common missteps.

Mistake #1: Denying Your Ethnic Background

If you deny your ethnic or racial background in order to fit into a corporation, you relinquish your competitive edge. One of your differentiating characteristics and strengths is that you hail from a distinctive culture and background, and to downplay or ignore that background is counterproductive. Just as high school students applying to college need to highlight their unique backgrounds and differentiating characteristics, you can use your ethnic background as a competitive edge. Besides your undergraduate degree or MBA, your ethnic background and ability to help a company increase its profits from these emerging markets can serve as one of your strengths. So why deny it?

Mistake #2: Failing to Leverage Your Ethnic Background

Too many minority employees fail to seize the opportunities that loom in front of them. If you're working for a fragrance company and know that your African American friends are turning to a certain type of perfume, speak up. Don't keep your thoughts inside. Use your knowledge of what minority women are buying to help your company surge ahead. Just as Luis Nunez at Kellogg's helped sell more cereal in Latin America because he knew what Hispanics preferred in their cereal, use your knowledge of minority tastes, buying trends, and tendencies. Don't cut off your own access and fail to leverage your own ethnic background.

Mistake #3: Not Speaking Up

At too many companies, the minority audience is just overlooked. Everything at the company aims to attract the majority audience. The $1 trillion of potential buying power (in 2010) of Hispanics is neglected, and many marketing opportunities go untapped. Don't keep your thoughts inside. If you know that your company has ignored an entire marketplace, assert yourself. And do your research and homework to make your case about the dollars that minorities spend for a product or in a market niche.

Mistake #4: Tapping Your (Diverse) Ethnic Background
Without Looking at the Big Picture

Despite growing minority influence and buying power, most campaigns aimed at African Americans, Latinos, and Asians are often part of a larger campaign targeting a wide audience. If you try to appeal to minorities only, you could be missing the boat. Most major brands target minorities as part of their overall strategy to sell toothpaste, credit cards, or vacation packages. You must understand the overall strategy and fit minority marketing into the brand's overall approach. In some cases, however, brands are creating campaigns that do target minorities specifically.

Be bold and ask to spend time with the chief marketing officer. If the chief marketing officer is speaking at an event, attend it and introduce yourself.

Mistake #5: Growing Stale in Ethnic Marketing

Avoid the minefield of staying in ethnic marketing for twelve years and then finding it difficult to move up. Building a career in diversity or ethnic marketing can yield a satisfying, productive, and lucrative corporate life. But ethnic marketing has its limitations. If you use ethnic marketing as a stepping-stone to the next promotion, that's a positive. If you're perceived at the company as someone who can sell only to Latinos, and not to the majority and greater ethnic audience, it can curtail your career rather than boost it. Even if you're succeeding at ethnic marketing, try to immerse yourself in mainstream marketing. As we shared in chapter 3, start networking with majority professionals who are doing mainstream marketing and promotions. Insinuate yourself into those events and develop rapport. Leverage your ethnic multicultural background into a career that demonstrates selling to the widest market.

Relying on Your Minority Know-how

Only thirty-seven years old, Melvin P. Young became vice president and chief of corporate communications at UniWorld Group, one of the leading advertising firms that targets minorities. But already he has had a series of influential jobs, such as brand manager at Walt Disney World, marketing director at Time Inc., and senior product director at Johnson & Johnson. Young's ascent up the corporate ladder mirrors the rising stature of minority buying power and its influence on the entire American culture. "If you look at what's driving TV, music, and retail, the minority influence is staggering. It's not just rap stars exerting influence. Minority influence is driving the culture," he says.

Reaching the minority market requires a distinctive approach compared to what worked with majority audiences in the past. "The world has changed, and too many brand managers tend to be insular and parochial in their thinking," he says. Politely, Young is suggesting that most majority marketers don't have the foggiest notion how to reach minority audiences, particularly younger ones.

Though Young is reluctant to divulge any of his proprietary strategies, he hints that reaching the ever increasing eighteen-to-thirty-five minority audience requires tapping the Internet, finding ways to interact with the audience, and reaching an audience with a more limited attention span than baby boomers'. What Young brings to the corporate world is a new way of seeing marketing: understanding minority audiences, recognizing that minority audiences need to be reached in different ways than majority markets, and knowing that old-fashioned marketing vehicles will be less effective with eighteen- to thirty-five-year-old minority consumers.

After getting his MBA from Pennsylvania State University, Young started in 1988 as an account supervisor at Quaker Oats in Chicago. His role was to increase the sales of products such as Rice-A-Roni and Gravy Train in Oklahoma and Arkansas. Most of the supermarket managers that he encountered had never dealt with an African American account supervisor before. Young, however, prided himself in his ability to read people and sense what they wanted to buy. "You're in a sales role. What I brought to the table was the ability to connect with people at the retail level. Race is immaterial," he says, since it's all about finding ways to market your product, reach an audience, build rapport, and deliver the best possible product at the most cost-effective price. His first job did not entail appealing to minority audiences, but focused on building relationships with Quaker Oats' sellers, servicing accounts, and focusing on the strengths of its products.

Based on his success in that position, he was hired in the mid-1990s as a senior product director at Johnson & Johnson (J&J), and worked out of Fort Washington, Pennsylvania. In that capacity, he played an instrumental role in marketing Children's Tylenol, the leading brand in its segment, to African American and Hispanic audiences. J&J had recently acquired Children's Motrin, which was a leader in the ibuprofen category, and its sales were cutting into those of Children's Tylenol. One of his roles was to ensure that Children's Tylenol sales didn't cannibalize the revenue of Children's Motrin.

Do Your Homework and Focus on Research

But J&J, like most of corporate America, wasn't used to targeting minority audiences, which were overlooked in the marketplace. The most important task that Young had to accomplish was to convince his managers to rely on research to build a case to target minorities, a brand-new approach in the marketplace. Though pharmaceutical companies used considerable research, Young had to influence J&J senior managers to use Nielsen Media Research's data for minority families. That research made the case that Children's Tylenol was losing its minority family market share. Furthermore, Young's research showed that 4 million babies were born annually in the United States, and by 2010, 40 percent of those babies would be born to African American, Hispanic, and Asian parents. After buttressing his case with the primary research, he wrote a two-page memo describing what it would take to reach minority parents for Children's Tylenol to regain its market share.

At the outset, Young's suggestion was met with resistance. The company wasn't used to tailoring its message to minority audiences. "Initially, my memo was ignored. There was a lack of market intelligence and strategic thinking," he says. As Young started gathering data to build his case, his managers started seeing his point. In fact, Young demonstrated that Children's Tylenol sales had dropped 14 share points with African American families and 11.5 share points with Hispanic families. That resulted in a loss of $3 million in sales for J&J. That loss raised awareness at J&J and motivated it to target minority consumers.

"You need to focus on the data, prepare recommendations, and explain why marketing to African Americans and Hispanics makes good business sense," Young says. This campaign, Young believes, was the first time that Johnson & Johnson had conducted research on African American mothers.

Reaching Minorities Must Be Part of an Overall Strategy

When Young was involved in designing the strategy to reach minority audiences, he focused on tying his approach to reaching minority audiences into J&J's overall strategy. "And that was about safety and trust. When it comes to children, you have to use the medium to reestablish credibility and trust," he says.

Within that overall campaign, Young devised a strategy to target minority mothers. Young recognized that minority families were often headed by single mothers who buy children's aspirin to reduce their children's fever. "The crux of the campaign revolved around educating African American and Hispanic mothers on how to manage fever," Young explains. Furthermore, reaching them required a multifaceted approach that used direct mail, spot ads on television, and radio and print advertisements. Since J&J was able to raise its market share with minority audiences, the campaign was successful. It also helped establish Young's career as a minority marketer who knew how to do research, make his case, and reach minority audiences.

Understanding the Minority Psychology

As a brand manager at Walt Disney World in Lake Buena Vista, Florida, from 1997 to 1999, Young was hired to introduce Disney's Wide World of Sports complex to the world. An extension of its theme parks, Disney's Wide World of Sports was a sports complex comprising a resort, the site of the annual Choice Awards, the location of the NFL Challenge series, the site of an annual tennis tournament, and the home of the Harlem Globetrotters, and was a place where families could play baseball and football, and relax together. Young's challenge was to market this new sports complex to minority families.

One of the keys to devising this strategy involved understanding the minority mind-set toward taking vacations. Research showed that minority families often took multifamily vacations, much more so than majority vacationers. Brothers, sisters, siblings, cousins, would take their vacation together with their children. Marketing Disney's Wide World of Sports as a destination vacation that included a resort, shopping, and athletic activities underscored the entire campaign. "Research is critical," Young says. "It sets the foundation for everything else."

To reach minority families, Young and his team devised a marketing campaign based around the Cunningham Family Reunion, two fictitious prototypical African American families that vacation at the Disney's Wide World of Sports complex. The campaign was seen through the eyes of a young black girl, Cunningham's daughter, and included sections of her diary in the print campaign, which appeared in *Ebony* and *Essence*. It also included direct mail, and stressed that the complex was safe and clean, because research showed that those two factors were critical in how African American families chose a vacation.

"Just as a company like Disney would devise a marketing plan for an international audience, this campaign created a multicultural marketing plan aimed at African American audiences," Young says. The campaign was very successful, exceeding its goals by 10 percent. It proved Young's ability to capture the multicultural audience, and catapulted him into his next challenge, at the UniWorld Group.

At UniWorld, Young spearheaded efforts at marketing to minorities, which was taking place in a whole new landscape. "Budgets are shifting dramatically. Internet budgets are rising by 12 to 15 percent a year. Reaching minorities and building word of mouth is different from what it was ten years ago," Young emphasizes.

Because Young was making a name for himself in minority marketing, he was often recruited by executive search firms. He used his Walt Disney, Time Inc., and Johnson & Johnson experience to snare a career opportunity at UniWorld. Like most executives who want to move up, Young also had to transplant, in his case from Chicago (Quaker Oats), to Milford, Connecticut (Frito-Lay), to Lake Buena Vista, Florida (Walt Disney), to New York, where he currently works.

One of his most invigorating challenges in 2006 involves reestablishing the Lincoln Mercury brand, which has suffered over the last ten years. Once Lincoln was known as a prestige car, mentioned in the same breath with Cadillac. But just as Cadillac had to be relaunched several years ago, after its sales and reputation suffered, so did Lincoln in 2006.

Selling automobiles to African Americans, Latinos, and other minorities in the United States requires understanding their perceptions when searching for a car. Research shows that most minority auto buyers invariably feel that dealers charge them more and slight them when they're looking for cars. To regain their trust, Lincoln hired Magic Johnson as the auto's spokesperson. It's also launching an interactive Web site that will be positioned at Black Planet and AOL Black Voices, sites that cater to African American audiences. "Over 4 percent of all auto buyers come to buy the car via an Internet lead," Young says.

Establish Word of Mouth or Face the Consequences

Young underscores one point about the minority audience that makes it different from the mainstream one. When a marketer is debuting a product that is aimed at minorities, how it introduces that product is critical. If the marketer makes a mistake at the outset, it can destroy the selling of the product. Word of mouth in the minority community is very strong because of the buzz created by the Internet, talk radio, the minority press, and direct mail. If a misstep is made at the outset, word of mouth can destroy the product. "First and foremost, you must establish credibility and word of mouth on the street. The first three things you do to introduce a project must be strategic, positioned correctly, and well thought out. The biggest thing with African Americans is word of mouth," Young says.

Often when Young attended marketing meetings, he was the only minority in the room. How was he able to convince his majority counterparts that a minority marketing strategy was necessary? "You have to lay out your business case. You have to make sure it's inclusive, fits into the company's plan, and connects with different market segments. I emphasize the lifetime value of people of color for the business. Minority customers tend to be loyal and can last a lifetime," he says.

Develop a Core Competency

By climbing the corporate ladder and changing jobs, Young developed a core competency in ethnic marketing. First he became an expert in marketing, learning how to deal with mainstream audiences, focusing on dealing with mainstream clients. Then he branched out to become an expert in minority marketing, though he always worked at leading firms that appeal to mass audiences. That is, he started out as a generalist and then became a specialist. Young exemplifies how a bright, ambitious minority professional can turn his ethnic background into a competitive edge, and use it to help mainstream companies reach minority and mainstream markets. He continually rose up the corporate ladder, from marketing associate, to senior assistant product director, to brand manager, to marketing director, to vice president and chief of corporate communications. Clearly his ascent is continuing, showing how Young's developing a strategic blueprint paid off.

Taking the Initiative

When Monica Pool Ross, who was profiled in chapter 5, was in HR at GTE, she knew the telecommunications company was trying to diversify its staff and build its market share with minority customers. But the company hadn't hired many minorities and didn't have a clear strategy. She made a case in a written presentation to her manager to develop a strategy to recruit more talented and educated African Americans. She positioned GTE to the National Black MBA Association (www.nbmbaa.org) as a technical company with cutting-edge technologies that would appeal to them. Ross was able to bring in a number of African American MBAs that helped move GTE into a better position to expand its minority audience.

While Ross had to justify for her manager the cost of recruiting, it was her initiative that paved the way. She didn't wait for someone to ask her to do it, but seized the opportunity to turn her ethnic background into a competitive edge, which helped her company expand.

Having a Global Perspective Helps

At forty years old, Cheryl McCants accepted the role of director of marketing services at the *New York Times*. Previously she served as a director and project manager at AT&T, and director of communications at Nike for Brand Jordan. A Brown University graduate who holds an M.S. in broadcast journalism from the Columbia University Graduate School of Journalism, she is an African American woman who has tapped her global experience. As a teenager, she lived in Bogota, Colombia, and she is bilingual. When she applied for her first job out of college, her fluency in Spanish helped her nail the job of international sales executive at AT&T. That job required her to increase long-distance sales to Spanish-speaking businesses. In fact, she concentrated on contacting Hispanic chambers of commerce to help increase business.

In her view, her African American background boosts her competency. "It helped me understand the various idiosyncrasies of the different communities. Having been raised as an African American and having lived in Bogota, I could relate to different lifestyles and understand the business culture," McCants says.

Turning Your Ethnicity into a Competitive Edge

AT&T faced a crisis in 1994. A cartoon that appeared in one of its internal newsletters showed a caricature of an African American person as a monkey. AT&T reacted by looking for a minority communications expert to improve dialogue internally. Since McCants had hosted a regional cable TV show on minority issues, it led to her being named public relations manager at AT&T consumer markets. Her ethnic background, ability to speak Spanish, and broadcast journalism background all played a role in winning the job.

McCants's multifaceted role revolved around crisis management. She helped devise a comprehensive strategic plan to refocus and redefine how minorities were treated at AT&T, and how the external minority community would be approached. In addition, a diversity director was hired at a vice-presidential level to address minority concerns, both internally and externally. McCants met with the African American community to inform them of what AT&T had been doing to help the minority community. She helped convince AT&T to target more marketing at minorities and step up its recruiting of minorities, and worked with the minority staff at AT&T to inform them of changes. She organized a meeting that included Percy Sutton, CEO of Inner City Broadcasting, to show how AT&T treated its minority employees, which helped rebuild the company's image. "My role tapped into my ability to communicate with the minority community. Because I knew that AT&T wasn't a racist company, I could use my conviction to influence others," McCants says.

Expand Your Vision Beyond Your Own Ethnic Group

Having succeeded in her role at AT&T, McCants moved on in 1999 to her next challenge, as director of communications for Brand Jordan at Nike, based in Beaverton, Oregon. She stayed in that position until 2001. Introducing the very snappy Brand Jordan sneakers, which sold for as much as $150, required an understanding of marketing "to a hip urban audience. We were trying to sell sneakers to as many people as possible. It had nothing to do with selling to African Americans or Latinos," she says. Nike knew its audience: hip, urban, trendy people, many of whom were majority and some of whom were ethnic. So Nike created buzz in urban markets in New York and Philadelphia, which created word of mouth that boosted Brand Jordan sales. "If you were hip, cool, and a trendsetter, we were appealing to you," McCants says.

Facing a Tough Challenge

But McCants never wanted to linger in a job and always sought the next challenge. During her tenure as director of marketing services at the *New York Times,* McCants faced a great challenge: boosting the single sales copies of the *New York Times* at a time when readers of newspapers were declining and people aged twenty-one to thirty-five were turning to the Internet for news. "My job entailed trying to sell more copies of the newspaper to audiences that hadn't been fully reached. If we didn't, we'd lose a huge business opportunity. My job was to demonstrate that this paper had a relevancy for everyone. There was something in it for everyone," she says.

Master Two Markets at Once

What McCants's experience shows is that minority employees have to keep their eyes on two targets at once. She became an expert at communications at AT&T, handling internal communications, and then moved on to Nike and handled external marketing. In both roles, her acumen in marketing and sensitivity to minority audiences contributed to her success. Both were integral to her moving up the corporate ladder. At Nike she contributed to creating hip, trendy marketing that led to Brand Jordan being a breakthrough product that appealed to diverse audiences. At the same time, her knowledge of the minority psyche contributed to her skill set. As a minority professional, no matter what product you're specializing at, you're tapping your minority expertise and using that know-how to reach both minority and majority audiences.

Discovering Your Identity

When Cynthia Park was four years old in the late 1960s, her father, who was in the export-import business, moved his family from South Korea to Marietta, Georgia, a suburb of Atlanta. Growing up, Park's focus was on assimilating to the mainstream culture. Fitting in was the driving force in her upbringing, as it is for most immigrant children. But now Park, who is forty-one years old and an executive vice president and managing director at Kang & Lee Advertising, uses her knowledge of the American and Asian cultures to target the Asian American market.

Though she spoke no English when she arrived in the U.S., within months she and her younger sister had acquired the language and could speak English by the time they started kindergarten. But in most of her classes, Park was the only Asian. Like most children, Park wanted to be well liked, sought friends, and desired the same toys that other, majority girls sought. Park did well in school, had many friends, and managed to fit in, but it wasn't until her late twenties that she "discovered my own ethnicity."

Kang & Lee Advertising, a global advertising firm, started in 1985 as one of the first firms specializing in emerging markets, including Asian American marketing. Joining the firm in 1993, Park worked on the account of AT&T, whose markets were changing because of deregulation and consumer choice in telephone companies.

"All of a sudden the immigrant market was playing a major role. Consumers got to choose their telecommunications service and how much they wanted to pay," Park says.

Understand Your Own Ethnic Group to Increase Sales

Despite the fact that she was raised in the United States, Park has a very close extended Korean family. Many of them continue to live in Korea, yet they stay in touch by telephone. When she started working on the AT&T account, she thought about how her Korean tradition was kept alive by calling cousins and aunts and uncles back home in Korea. Part of the AT&T campaign that was marketed to six international locales emphasized that calling home was a way of maintaining cultural traditions. Park could draw on her personal immigrant experience to help shape the campaign. Hence, the commercial emphasized calling home to stay in touch with one's family, something most immigrants could relate to.

On a subsequent assignment, the Allstate insurance account, Park faced different obstacles selling the product to the Asian American market. Taking out personal life insurance was not something that most Asian families did. Therefore, the Allstate marketing campaign first had to instill a reason why families needed insurance, and then had to reinforce Allstate's "good hands" advertisements and build name recognition for the Asian families not used to the product. Knowing and understanding the culture helped Park to frame and shape the Allstate marketing plan. "You can bring insights to the table because you've lived their life. You know who your target audience is because they're just like your family," she says.

On the other hand, being of the same ethnic background as your target audience can be a trap. Park recalls one copywriter, who hailed from a Chinese background, who wrote copy for a campaign based exactly on her life. But the writing was so ethnocentric and parochial that it didn't resonate with most Asian American audiences and was rejected. "You need to look at appealing to ethnic audiences from a broader perspective and recognize that you may not represent the masses," Park says.

Becoming a Minority Specialist

I've already noted in several chapters that minority marketing can be a trap, but it's only a trap if you let it limit your advancement. Park's ascent demonstrates that becoming an expert in ethnic marketing can be a stepping-stone to becoming an executive vice president and managing director. She's leveraged her expertise in Asian marketing as a differentiating characteristic, which has allowed her to run her own agency within a global advertising firm. She's been so skillful at succeeding at major nationwide advertising and marketing campaigns for Fortune 500 clients and contributing to their bottom line that she has been rewarded with several promotions. While ethnic marketing can still be a trap, Park proves that it can also be a launching pad.

Because she has been so successful in helping create marketing campaigns for major brands, Park can use those skills to transfer into mainstream marketing, if she so desires. Once you master the cultural specialty, you can transfer into a larger media firm. Park has been able to leverage her own ethnic background, forge a specialty that helps her global advertising company meet its customers' need, and tap into her own roots as well.

If you are specializing in minority marketing, I recommend making inroads into mainstream marketing. Volunteer to work on a campaign that goes beyond Asian American or African American campaigns. Many organizations do matrix marketing, where many people play a role in an overall campaign, so getting involved in mainstream shouldn't be that difficult.

Meeting the Needs of a Changing Marketplace

In the mid-1980s, when Berlinda Fontenot-Jamerson had already been a community involvement manager at the Southern California Gas Company for fifteen years, she and a team of three other professionals thought the time was right for this utility company to begin a diversity initiative and target the growing minority audiences of California. Up until that time, the utility, which turned into Sempra Energy in the late 1990s after deregulation was introduced, had not launched any diversity initiatives. The team of four devised a brief proposal and presented it to Dick Farman, the utility's recently named CEO. Though he was intrigued by it, he returned it to them, asking for more information on how the diversity group would add to the company's bottom line.

The quartet strengthened its pitch, explaining how deregulation would alter the utility landscape. "It behooved us to understand the changing needs of the marketplace versus the backdrop of deregulation when people have a choice. If we want to be regarded as a service provider of choice, we can't offer the same kind of vanilla product," Fontenot-Jamerson asserts. By creating marketing campaigns that appeal to minority audiences and being more sensitive to their needs, Sempra could boost its revenue. CEO Farman liked their revision and authorized a diversity department.

Yet, even then, Fontenot-Jamerson and her three colleagues faced obstacles. Farman authorized the new department but delivered no budget for it; selected as director a vice president of human resources who was minority but didn't fully understand diversity's implications; and provided no staff. Without a staff, without a budget, and without a clear mandate, the diversity area floundered, and its new director left after six months. Asked to replace her predecessor, Fontenot-Jamerson initially declined because she knew that without a budget, she was being set up for failure. Finally, after she explained why the office of diversity needed a budget and staffing, her requests were granted, and she had a budget and one administrative assistant to begin accomplishing many tasks.

Offices of diversity are fairly new divisions that corporations have established to improve their minority hiring and how minority employees are treated. Most fall under human resources, but some report directly to the company's CEO. When a diversity director is immediately responsible to a CEO, not HR, he or she usually carries more influence. It's considered a staffing job, not a profit-making or business one. At some companies, the diversity director can exert solid influence, but at others, it's more about window dressing and trying to please EEOC regulators.

Overcoming the Obstacles

One of the major impediments that Fontenot-Jamerson, who is sixty years old and was named director of diversity at ABC in March 2005, faced at the Southern California Gas Company when she was launching the office of diversity was the antagonism that many majority employees felt toward affirmative action. "Most people," she says, "think diversity is affirmative action wrapped in a new tuxedo." But she spent much of her time at the outset educating the utility's staff about the differences between affirmative action and diversity. Affirmative action involved complying with laws mandated by the government, whereas diversity was a corporate initiative that leveraged its minority employees and found ways to appeal to a changing demographic.

Furthermore, she spent considerable time reassuring the mostly male majority audience that the office of diversity would not thwart their rise up the corporate ladder, their greatest fear. How did she persuade them? "I found majority men who would champion the diversity cause," she replies succinctly. Fontenot-Jamerson stressed that the goals of the office of diversity were focused on strengthening the company's bottom line more than fighting racism.

During her ten years in charge of the office of diversity, the department contributed to making Sempra Energy rank highest (or near the top) in several customer-service ratings. Because Sempra reached out to minority communities, its ratings were high with minority audiences, unusual for a utility. When she left the office of diversity at Sempra Energy, she had six vice presidents working for her and an administrative assistant, showing how the department's impact and influence had grown from the beginning.

Fontenot-Jamerson illustrates how her office reached out to the community by noting that Sempra created a consumer advisory council, which consisted of several minority members. When its many Vietnamese customers were having problems trying to heighten their natural gas flames, it was leading to safety issues. But Vietnamese would not permit Sempra's utility workers to enter their homes in their metal boots, and utility laws in California prevented them from being able to remove them. Finally, the Vietnamese member of the consumer advisory council suggested that the utility workers wear surgical booties over their boots, which solved the problem.

Having recently earned a pension after working at Sempra Energy for nearly thirty years, Fontenot-Jamerson didn't have to continue working. But she felt that the director of diversity position at ABC offered her the opportunity to accomplish more of her "passion," which involves helping diversity efforts in the company. She wanted to "create a workforce that matches the demographics in California, where the minority has become the majority."

What is the mission of Disney's office of diversity? Fontenot-Jamerson replies that it's "developing a strategic plan for diversity." Her office provides "counseling, coaching, and technical support to management and employees on implementing diversity initiatives throughout the company." Her office is part of the HR department and a staff function.

Asserting Your Identity Can Pay Off

Fontenot-Jamerson's experience proves that taking risks can pay off in moving up the corporate ladder. When she was at Southern California Gas, she and her colleagues could easily have maintained the status quo, kept their mouths shut, and not tried to initiate an office of diversity. But she saw a reason to speak up, took the plunge, suggested that the company devise a marketing strategy to appeal to an emerging minority marketplace at a time of deregulation, and ultimately, she was rewarded.

Furthermore, Fontenot-Jamerson was not afraid to speak up in the corporate world and essentially say, "Here I am, a strong, outspoken African American woman and I think I can help move this company forward, treat its minority employees differently, and reach out to our minority customers." Instead of denying her identity, she used it to improve the company and also boost her own career.

Action Steps

- Before you join the company, conduct due diligence to see if it does targeted marketing to Latinos, African Americans, Asians, and other minorities. If not, find out why. If you decide to work at the company, consider starting a campaign to reach out to minorities.

- As Melvin Young describes in forceful terms, "research is key." Do your homework. Learn how many minorities are buying mutual funds from your financial-services company, lawn mowers from Home Depot or Lowe's DVD players from Best Buy or Circuit City, and how many aren't. What will it take to get them to buy? What will it take to reach them via a marketing campaign?

- Be sensitive to your roots. If you hail from a Caribbean background and notice that the tiny jerk chicken shack in your neighborhood is attracting standing-room crowds every night, might there be a franchise possibility? If you are Indian and you notice that a certain type of Indian pastel skirt is selling at a local store and you work for Ann Taylor, might you suggest it as a sportswear item?

- Ask your minority friends what motivates them to choose a financial-services or insurance company, buy an automobile, or choose a vacation. Use that informal

research, supported by more formal research, to help your
company market its products to minorities.

- Also keep in mind how the minority campaign will fit
into the brand's overall strategy, as Melvin Young did when
he marketed Children's Tylenol.

- Use your contacts and associations to further your career.
When GTE needed to hire a more diversified staff,
Monica Pool Ross recruited at the National Black MBA
Association, which yielded positive results from the
company.

- If you do secure a job in ethnic marketing, keep your
options open, your networking and antennae active,
and also get involved in mainstream campaigns.
Don't wake up ten years later and find yourself trapped
in the same job that you started with. Keep stretching
your talents.

- Learn to take risks on the job. When Berlinda Fontenot-
Jamerson and her colleagues noticed that their utility
company was going to have to market its service to an
increasing minority clientele, they suggested the
company inaugurate a diversity department. Though
they encountered initial resistance, the department
came to play a forceful role at the company.

- If you feel like an outsider, use that to help your
company. Companies are constantly seeking creative
solutions to broaden their product line, whether it's a
new mop cleaner, air bags for cars, or distilled water
with fruit flavors.

- Leverage your ethnicity to boost your career while keeping your company's goals in the forefront. That's what Cheryl McCants accomplished by helping to create Brand Jordan as a trendy sneaker that appealed to ethnics and the majority audience who wanted to be hip.

7

MAKING THE LEAP INTO THE
CORPORATE SUITE

■

YOU'VE BEEN NAMED a vice president and you're feeling
good. You followed your strategic career blueprint, surrounded
yourself with mentors, did your networking, and outperformed your
colleagues. You've been making all the right moves, and your strategies are paying off. Your responsibilities have been increased, your
salary has increased dramatically, you're eligible for bonuses, and
you're making an impact on increasing your company's revenue.
You're primed for moving up.

Yet from my point of view, you're only at the starting gate. Your
work has just begun. If you rest on your laurels and begin to coast,
you will grind to a halt. If you've mastered corporate politics, learned
how to schmooze, and gained the confidence of your superiors, your
politicking has just started. Getting into the executive suite entails
making all the right moves. You must make sure you've reached out
to all the major influencers and decision makers, and be as polished as

you can be. Any rough edges can cost you a promotion. One confrontation at an executive meeting in which you alienate a senior executive can cause you to fall off the succession plan. If you avoid networking with a senior manager on one of the three essential committees (promotion, executive, and leadership), it can mean the difference between your ascension and your rival's promotion. One mistake and you will be like the chess player who moves a queen into jeopardy and loses the match. Moving up the corporate ladder as the pyramid and organizational chart shrinks means you must play to win, cover all bases, strategize your every move, and become a spectacular, not just outstanding, performer.

As you begin to rise up the corporate ladder, the politics begin to change. You need to view things from a 360-degree perspective. You need to take care of the little details while focusing on the big picture. When you were named a vice president, you had to develop strong peer relationships, maintain a solid relationship with your boss and his or her boss, satisfy your customers, and fit into the company's overall goals. As you draw closer to the executive suite, the politics intensify. Your chess playing needs to ascend to another level, and you need to become more aware of where you fit in the company's overall goals and its succession plan. You'll have to operate like a grandmaster, not just a competent chess player. And you must be aware at all times of who the players are: who is close to the CEO, whom the HR director leans on, whom the CFO goes to for assistance.

In sum, you need to become more strategic.

Superior performance is a constant thread that will catapult you forward. But performance is only one factor among many. You need to be able to demonstrate a multitude of characteristics beyond performance, including having charisma, possessing superior presentation skills, being able to think on your feet, and being able to out-strategize your competitors. If you're in the financial area and know that the CFO will be retiring next year, you have to plan your moves to be considered to replace him. Who exactly is on the promotion or executive leadership committee that you need to impress? What projects can you get involved in or initiate that will enable you to boost profits, show your financial skills, ensure that you get noticed, and propel you forward as a likely successor? How can you make a name for yourself at the company? What skills do you need to acquire to enhance your tool kit? Which of your competitors will you have to outdo to leap ahead of him or her?

You need to think like a colonel in the armed forces who is leading his or her soldiers into war and wants to be considered for a promotion to general. How do I become the best possible leader? How do I impress the Joint Chiefs of Staff? How do I make sure the generals at the Pentagon know what I've accomplished in the field? How do I differentiate myself from the other colonels?

I've already cited how important networking and mentoring are to your eventual succession. At the senior levels, networking and mentoring assume a whole new dimension. You constantly have to schmooze senior leaders, attend innumerable business conferences, off-sites, get-togethers, and cocktail parties, and prove that you belong. CEOs such as Richard Parsons, Stan O'Neal, Andrea Jung, and Ken Chenault could discuss any corporate strategy with any senior leader at any Time Warner, Merrill Lynch, Avon, or American Express business meeting, strategy session, or cocktail party to prove that they belong. None would have risen to become CEO if they were socially ill at ease and unable to network, gain the confidence of the current CEOs, and impress each member of the executive team. It was their social adroitness as well as their superior performance that contributed to their success.

"I think life is about doing the best that you can with what you are born with," Stan O'Neal, CEO of Merrill Lynch, once told the *Harvard Alumni* magazine. O'Neal's MBA from Harvard Business School played a role in his ascent. But he didn't join Merrill until 1986, when he was thirty-six years old, after having served as assistant treasurer at General Motors. Once at Merrill, he advanced rapidly to become head of capital markets, cohead of the corporate and institutional group, and CFO. Known for staying in the office most nights until ten o'clock, he gained the trust of David Komansky, Merrill's former CEO, his godfather. That trust, combined with the fact that he raised pretax profits from 22 to 28 percent when he was president and COO, catapulted him to CEO.

When you're a minority professional, moving up to the corporate suite entails proving that you belong. You will be questioned. Do you have enough polish and know-how? Can you deal with the board of directors and analyze a company's balance sheet if your company needs to acquire another company? Can you oversee downsizing if the company needs to shrink? Can you make the tough decisions? Have you led a major acquisition or brand marketing campaign to demonstrate that you have what it takes to succeed? Because you're African American, Hispanic, Asian, or a woman, people will ask: do you have the guts, the inner fortitude, the chutzpah, to make the tough decisions and still be a positive, energetic leader? You'll have to prove yourself again and again and never let down your performance.

Making it into the executive suite as a managing director or senior vice president is equivalent to running a marathon. Just like running that twenty-six-mile race, you must have the fortitude and stamina to last long distances, maintain your performance and never let it down for the entire race, be confident throughout, stay energetic the entire course, and always focus on your ultimate target. Just as in marathon racing, you need to train exhaustively and do your homework in order to move up to the ranks of senior executive.

But your sense of timing is critical. You need to read the corporate tea leaves to see where the company is going. If the firm is moving toward international sales, you need to strike a deal overseas or forge a relationship with partners overseas to ensure that you help the company achieve its goal. If the company is cutting costs, you have to be a leader in finding new ways to reduce overhead. If you're developing a new business, you can seize the day and take a leadership role in getting that done. And you have to make sure that your bosses are aware that you're leading this effort, without appearing overly self-serving or self-aggrandizing. You're juggling numerous balls in the air, walking fine lines, and showing incredible finesse and dexterity to get noticed *and* get the job done.

Mistake #1: Becoming Overconfident

I have seen innumerable minority professionals who have been promoted to vice president make this mistake. They think that the world owes them a living, and that now they can coast to gain the next promotion. Overconfident vice presidents who sit back and think the world will come to them and that promotions will happen naturally because they possess an MBA are doomed to failure. This is not the time to let down your guard, but it is an opportunity to step up your performance, be visible at leadership conferences, and acquire new skills that will make you more marketable. The more strategic your thinking, the more you can position yourself to move up. But if you think your one raise and promotion will guarantee your rise up the corporate ladder, you will have deluded yourself to the point that it can actually lead to your downfall.

Mistake #2: Letting Your Performance Suffer

You have your new vice president business cards. You feel as if you're on top of the world. You've notified your mom and dad, siblings and first cousins, and everyone knows that you've made it. But once you've made it and have been promoted, you can lose it. The Achilles' heel of most minority professionals who overcome many hurdles to be named a vice president is they let their performance lapse. They think they have it made. If you rest on your laurels and don't work as hard as you did when clawing your way up the ladder, it can lead to your being terminated. Being named a vice president is a form of recognition for your accomplishments and hard work, but that diligence and conscientiousness must be sustained. Use your promotion to boost your performance, make yourself hungrier, and intensify your dedication. Look for new ways to help the company and yourself.

Mistake #3: Playing It Safe

Now that you've risen up the corporate ladder, you think you can play it safe. You avoid taking risks and don't want to make a mistake that will hurt your reputation. That's the antithesis of what I'd recommend. Melvin Young, the marketing professional from UniWorld Group profiled in the previous chapter, exemplifies how taking risks and building your skills can result in moving up the ladder step-by-step.

Having gained a soupçon of recognition, begin thinking about becoming a risk taker. Find projects that you can get involved in to boost the company's profit, lead the firm into new ventures, and make a name for yourself. Al Zollar, the IBM executive who was profiled in chapter 5, "Strengthening Your Performance," took risks and accepted assignments that most others avoided. Meeting those challenges made a name for Zollar, which led to his becoming general manager of the $2 billion IBM software division. Without that risk taking, he might still be slogging away as an IBM middle manager instead of one of its premiere business leaders. Playing it safe leads to staying in place and going nowhere, and that frequently triggers the minority professional's leaving the company after five to seven years when he sees his career has stalled.

Mistake #4: Not Possessing the Intangible Skills

By the time you've advanced to be a vice president and are vying for a senior position, you're competing with a host of other qualified candidates. In most cases, all possess the technical skills. If you're vying to become CFO, you'll master everything you need to know, from balance sheets to Sarbanes-Oxley. Those won't be your differentiating characteristics. What separates one candidate from another is the intangible skills, not the technical ones.

Many of those intangible skills revolve around communication. Signs of being a superior communicator include the ability to make a dynamic presentation; answering difficult questions adroitly, and being spontaneous, natural, and flexible rather than stiff and unyielding. Being a communicator also involves all the interpersonal skills, which corporations erroneously refer to as "soft skills" (there's nothing soft about them; in fact, they're difficult to achieve), which involve leading people, motivating staff, and reading people's emotional makeup.

I recall a situation where two vice presidents were vying to become senior vice president of finance at a large financial-services company. Both were interviewed for its in-house magazine, which was circulated to all global employees. One candidate went with the flow, and one was inflexible. The more flexible VP agreed to be photographed looking like the Statue of Liberty, while the other one refused. In addition, the flexible candidate delivered great quotes, and three-quarters of the article was devoted to his comments. When the article was published, everyone figured the flexible one was going to be named CFO because he was prominently positioned on the cover and most of the article was about him. Both were equally qualified in technical skills, but the flexible one showed superior communication skills. Sure enough that article became a factor in his ascension, and he was named senior VP. The other one soon left the company.

If your public speaking skills are lacking, get assistance. Go to Toastmaster International (www.toastmasters.org). Hire a coach (consider the Coach Federation, www.coachfederation.org, or the Worldwide Association of Coaches, www.wabccoaches.com, as we noted in the introduction). Gain experience speaking at conferences and off-sites. Hire a media consultant. It'll pay off when you get the nod and overtake a competitor.

Mistake #5: Letting the Old Boys' Network Get to You

During work, most of your colleagues and bosses accept you. After work, you may not be invited to play golf at the suburban country club or even asked for the after-work beer at the nearby watering hole. Don't let those exclusions get you down. Form your own networking club, and invite like-minded thinkers for a beer, or play golf at the local public course with colleagues. Learn to play golf and join a country club that is open to diversity. Accentuate your strengths. As stated in previous chapters, brand yourself as the best possible marketer, accountant, or strategist at the company to offset your lack of connections at the golf course or watering hole. You can overcome the old boys' network.

Surmount the Unwritten Code

In the past, many minorities were selected as middle managers but few were chosen as vice presidents or leaders. It was almost as if senior executives treated the corporate suite like their neighborhoods. If too many minorities moved in, property values would plummet, some thought. And if too many minorities gained power in the executive suite, they'd promote more minorities and conduct a palace coup. Hence, the majority held on to their power and promoted people who looked, thought, and acted like them.

But the code is changing. Companies have seen the effects of the burgeoning minority buying power and are responding by being more open to promoting more minorities into the corporate suite. To tap into that increasing buying power, corporations know they need talented executives who understand the growing Hispanic, African American, and Asian markets. Hence, opportunity is growing, despite the obstacles.

Anticipate the Scrutiny

Though corporations are increasingly open to seeking talented minorities for senior management positions, you will be scrutinized more than majority candidates will be. If a majority person makes a mistake, it's condoned, and the candidate will quickly bounce back, recover, learn from it, and advance. But if a minority vice president makes a mistake on an account, doesn't negotiate the highest price, makes a recommendation that goes awry, or doesn't deliver as promised, it can be the death knell of his or her career. Keeping that in mind, you have to stay on top of your game, do your homework, and prepare extensively in order to avoid any fatal miscues.

Tap into the CEO's Vision

In order to be considered for those prized senior vice president positions, you must buy into the vision of the CEO. At each company, the CEO operates differently. At JPMorgan Chase, CEO Jamie Dimon has been slashing expenses and costs. Up-and-coming leaders don't wait for directives, but downsize the staff and cut costs to gain his favor. At competitor Citigroup, which suffered several ethical scandals, Charles Prince, the CEO and its former general counsel, has eliminated many of the executives whose reputations were tarnished by the scandals and emphasized integrity over ruthlessness. Operating in an ethical way *and* boosting profits has become the standard for gaining promotions at Citigroup. Linking your goals to the CEO's and staying one step ahead of the CEO are ways to position yourself for advancement.

Overcome the "You're Not Ready Yet" Syndrome

When minority vice presidents are denied promotion to the next level, most senior majority executives withhold the real deal on why people of color are not advancing. Instead, minority professionals are stonewalled and told, "You're not ready yet." That becomes the all-inclusive but vague reason that keeps them in their place, trapped in their job, and locked out of the corporate corridors. Because "You're not ready yet" is an extremely subjective evaluation, it can mean many things, including (1) you actually lack the competencies that will enable you to function as a senior executive; (2) the company is not ready to promote talented minorities and fears the backlash it will cause in its majority ranks; and (3) you require more challenges to test your mettle and a wider range of experience before you are promoted again.

If you ask, "What do I need to do to get ready?" your question will be deflected or go unanswered. It'll be parried instead with half-hearted, amorphous responses such as "Go and ripen your experience," "Polish your performance," and "Expand your skill set." All of those responses are not very helpful and don't clue you in on what you need to do. What you need to do is find out from your trusted mentors and networking circle exactly what you have to do to climb the ladder to the next rung. What godfather do you need? What high-profile project do you need to land? How do you make a name for yourself without offending the senior executives? Whom do you need to impress? What leadership skills can you demonstrate? What's the next great corporate business area that will boost profits that you can get involved in? Or do you need to find another company and culture that will be more open to your strengths?

Read the Signs

If executive meetings are being held and you're not invited, find out why. If you're left out of the inner circle, ask around to see why you're not being included. Is a Western Union message being sent to you that you're not part of the succession plan, aren't considered executive material, and aren't recognized as a potential senior leader? If the signs are clear that you're on the outs, consider updating your résumé, contacting executive recruiters, and finding new options. If your current senior management doesn't appreciate your talents, another company's senior leadership team will.

Focus on Self-Initiating Projects;
Don't Wait to Be Anointed

If you're being left out of the loop, you have one other option besides contacting your local executive recruiting firm: making a name for yourself inside the company. If you can devise a strategy that can use your ethnicity as a competitive edge, develop a product targeted at African Americans, Latinos, women, or Asians that hasn't been done before, you can make a case for yourself to be promoted. Don't wait to be anointed. Be proactive and take risks. Find new markets. Devise revenue-producing schemes. Take leadership positions. Force the company into promoting you based on your accomplishments.

Possess the Entire Package of Skills

If there's one common thread among all the minority CEOs who have advanced to the top, it's that they possess the entire package: their performance is always outstanding; they work on high-profile projects that move the company forward; and they dress the role, look sharp, speak eloquently, think on their feet, and possess charisma— when they walk into a room, they are the magnet that attracts everyone's attention. If you intend to become a senior executive, you need coaching. You have to dress the part, become a dynamic speaker, and improve your listening skills; and if you weren't born with charisma, develop it. If you stammer when you speak at a conference, or rely on PowerPoint demonstrations that your audience can't decipher, it will hurt your chances of advancing.

Monitor Your Own Performance

Once you've been named a vice president, there are only so many other promotions you're going to receive. But you have to keep challenging yourself. You need to monitor your own growth in the corporation. Are you being asked to attend leadership weekends at the Aspen Institute or at Ivy League colleges? Are you being encouraged to speak at professional conferences and to lead discussions on the state-of-the-art products that your company is developing? If not, take the lead and try to initiate these invitations.

Without resting on your laurels, you have to keep growing and stretching your talents and expanding your skill set. If you've managed a group of ten, find out how you can manage a group of forty. If you're only managing people in the U.S., see if you can manage a cross-functional group that is global.

If you're situated at headquarters, get out into the field. Make sure the regional managers know you and are impressed by you. Open up communication. Avoid staying in a silo, i.e., just your own department, because those regional managers can make or break your reputation to the steering committee that will select the next senior vice president. Cover all your bases; don't slight anyone in a position of power. For that matter, build strong relationships with your peers and subordinates.

Confront the Old Boys' Network

After graduating from Dartmouth College in 1987, Robert D. Charles (now forty-one), an African American native of Washington, D.C., had opportunities galore. Companies were looking to diversify their staff and were seeking bright Ivy League minorities for their management-development programs. Since Charles was interested in the financial-services industry, he joined Chase Manhattan Bank's management-development program. He excelled in that program and was selected for one of the plum assignments, as an assistant treasurer at Chase Securities.

Though performance was one of the keys to being promoted, he noticed early on that several of his Italian American colleagues were invited to hockey games or after-work gatherings at the local pub. Charles and several of the women assistant treasurers never received those invitations. "The bonding and the preferential treatment" weren't bestowed on women or men of color, he said. Still, he thought that outstanding performance would be rewarded, even if he wasn't hoisting Budweisers after work with the division's director.

Form Your Own Network to Boost Your Career

When he met a majority trader on the securities floor who had also graduated from Dartmouth, Charles and he started to form a bond. He became one of Charles's mentors. But first his mentor checked to determine that Charles was an outstanding performer who was skilled at executing trades. Once he did the due diligence and noted that Charles was a superior performer, he took him under his wing. Even when a mentor finds you, it's your performance that lets you in the circle.

"That first connection can turn out to be very beneficial and life and career changing," Charles admits. He and his mentor would meet for an occasional dinner or beer. At one point his mentor told him, "You want to get closer to the money. In commercial banks, the guys that make the most money are the investment bankers or traders. That's where you want to be." His mentor offered to sponsor him in one of Chase's trading programs.

"In the corporate jungle, there are many folks that can become impediments or enablers," Charles notes. Finding the enablers and avoiding the impediments is crucial to moving up the ladder. Charles's mentor sponsored his career-development program, helped him surmount some of the obstacles, and supported him in joining programs that would boost his career. "Let me get you on the short list or in front of the decision makers," his mentor would tell him. "In order to be at the right place at the right time, you need someone who can help you take advantage of the opportunity," Charles learned.

But instead of seizing that opportunity, Charles felt that he needed to strengthen his competencies and business acumen. With his mentor writing him a strong recommendation, he applied to Harvard Business School and was accepted, and he earned his MBA in 1993.

What Charles Didn't Learn at Harvard Business School

At Harvard, Charles learned much about attacking any business problem through its case-study program. Earning that MBA enhanced his résumé, expanded his knowledge, and provided him with the skills that would lead him to the executive suite. But asked what he learned about moving up in the corporation in the Harvard MBA program, Charles replied, "I can't recall any explicit advice on how to move up, when to move, or why to move. Yet there was an unwritten expectation that all of us would become C-level executives," he said. By C-level executives, Charles refers to chief executive officer, chief financial officer, chief marketing officer, or chief of something.

Nor did he receive any specific assistance on how an African American can overcome the old boys' network. Whatever he mastered about that subject would be gleaned from on-the-job experience.

With his Harvard MBA on his résumé, Charles sought a job that would tap into his Spanish language expertise and offer global experience. He opted to become a consultant and case team leader at Bain & Company, based in Dallas, Texas. Most of the work out of the Dallas office was centered in Mexico. Charles concentrated on working in financial services, drawing on his Chase Manhattan Bank experience, and ventured into working for consumer product and transportation companies. He also expanded his technical expertise because Bain &

Company devised its own technology process and methodology. As a consultant, he was also gaining more business expertise, which he felt he needed to round out his skills.

At Bain & Company, Charles faced a different type of old boys' network than the one he had encountered at Chase. Since many of its chief executives, like Mitt Romney, who became the governor of Massachusetts, were Mormons, the culture tended to promote Mormons. "If you looked at the prime jobs, there was clearly a preponderance of Mormons," Charles explains.

Overcoming the Old Boys' Network

How did Charles overcome that old boys' network? He focused on excelling in the areas that he knew best, such as financial services. He worked hard to establish an expertise in that area and become as knowledgeable as possible and valuable to the company. Combining his acumen in financial services with his knowledge of Spanish and his growing expertise in the Mexican economy, he was building a repertoire of valuable strengths that set him apart from the other consultants.

Exploring One's Entrepreneurial Side

After three years at Bain & Company, expanding his knowledge, he opted out and went to work as president and chief operating officer at Advanced Device Corporation. That was a start-up company that was trying to raise $10 million to develop two patents that the company owned. Since Charles was interested in developing his entrepreneurial skills, this job enabled him to explore that aspect of his character, and not have to worry about bureaucracies and old boys' networks. After nearly a year of trying to raise funds, he couldn't achieve that goal. Charles left to become a partner at Computer Sciences Corporation (CSC), a technological consulting company that worked in Europe and the U.S.

Get Involved in a Breakthrough Project

At CSC Charles oversaw a team of financial professionals who were working on a very complex project, involving a large Spanish bank that was exploring whether to acquire a large Latin American bank to expand its business to a different continent. Charles managed a team of twenty-five professionals who conducted due diligence to determine if the deal made sense and the price was right. They finally determined that acquiring the bank was a sound investment, which led the Spanish bank to acquire it. This consulting assignment of exploring an acquisition and leading a team of twenty-five professionals on a deal that was worth millions of dollars catapulted Charles's career. It provided him with a breakthrough project that revealed many of his talents and prepared him for the next challenge.

This consulting project added depth to Charles's résumé. He demonstrated leadership on a multimillion-dollar acquisition. It proved that he was ready for a senior management position.

Having the Right Skills and the Right Timing

Soon after Charles had worked on this acquisition, Ford CEO Jack Nassar tried to shake up Ford in several ways. Nassar wanted to diversify its senior management ranks as Ford diversified its revenue stream to appeal to minority markets. An executive search firm was looking to hire an executive vice president at Ford Consumer Financial Services, its credit arm, who reported to the chairman and CEO of that division and served on its twelve-member executive leadership team. Charles interviewed for the job and was hired in 2000 as an executive VP. Only seven years after graduating with his MBA from Harvard Business School, Charles had entered the lofty executive offices of Ford, the country's second largest auto manufacturer after General Motors.

He attributed his landing this position to his credentials, his experience, and his timing. "Nassar wanted to bring in new blood to the company and was willing to pay top dollar for it. He wanted youthful thinking and wanted to change that thirty-plus-year legacy of most of its executives. His focus was on future planning, and how we take our $29 billion in cash, and invest in our core business in the future," Charles says. At age thirty-six, Charles was youthful; he could help appeal to diverse markets, had proven that he could analyze an acquisition, and carried that prestigious Harvard MBA. He had even been heavily involved in e-commerce at his previous position, and Ford recognized that many young buyers searched the Web before going to the auto showroom.

Early in Charles's career at Ford, he ran up against obstacles. Though he was a member of the executive leadership team, which consisted of a dozen senior executives in that division, his immediate boss, the CEO of Ford Financial, surrounded himself with a team of yes men. These yes men never questioned what their CEO said, never raised issues, and acceded to whatever he said. But Charles, who had a solid relationship with his boss, didn't feel comfortable acquiescing in everything his boss said and asked pointed, thoughtful questions about the business strategy. Often he was the only one of the executive team who would ask questions. After several of these meetings, his colleagues would congratulate him on the questions that he raised, but no one followed suit or asked questions themselves. Charles managed to ingratiate himself with the boss, perform well, and excel at various activities, including scoring highest in Capstone, an internal management-development program, but never felt fully accepted on the job.

Dealing with his CEO was one of his most difficult obstacles, which may have had little to do with his being a minority. If you kowtow to your boss and don't raise questions, you're viewed as a lackey, aren't showing leadership, and can't be considered as upper-senior-management material. At the same time, by speaking up and not being a yes man, you're perceived as a threat, and that can have repercussions. Polonius in Shakespeare's *Hamlet* says "to thine own self be true," and Charles lived up to that advice. Whether or not he paid a price for it is arguable.

During the beginning of Charles's third year on the job in 2003, Ford was undergoing major difficulties. Its Explorer SUV was involved in numerous accidents, the Firestone tire controversy had damaged its reputation, and its market share was declining due to competition from Honda, Toyota, and Nissan. When CEO Nassar was forced out and replaced by insider Bill Ford, the impetus to hire and promote minority candidates subsided. Within months, Charles was feeling excluded and slighted, and looked to make a change. He received a decent buyout and left to run his own company, North Star

Advisors in West Bloomfield, Michigan, which raises capital for companies and provides management consulting to middle-market firms.

Make the Necessary Adjustments

Charles learned that a senior corporate executive must constantly adjust "his personal aspirations to fit the company's business objectives," he said. He also learned that you can't fully control your own career, that a change of CEO in the executive suite can alter overnight a company's vision, its operating model, and the way it treats its employees. "At all times, you have to know who the decision makers are, where you stand in succession planning, know what your contribution is and how you add value to the company's business model," he says. Had Nassar, a proponent of diversity, remained as CEO, Charles contends, he'd likely still be at Ford as an executive vice president.

Charles wonders if he made all the right political moves. Had he been less outspoken, would senior management have treated him better? On the other hand, he's an inquisitive individual who relies on facts, and he asked questions to move the company forward. All of his questions aimed to strengthen Ford, which was facing a series of problems, not to damage it. Were there other executives he could have reached out to and formed alliances with? Was he excluded because he wasn't part of the old boys' network? Charles can only guess at the answers.

Going Beyond Technical Competence

When Mary A. Winston, the forty-four-year-old executive vice president and chief financial officer of New York–based Scholastic Inc. (known for publishing the Harry Potter books in the U.S.), was working on her MBA at Northwestern University, she expected that the combination of technical competence and possessing the right credentials would enable her to advance. In fact, her technical know-how, MBA, and competence have enabled her to climb up the corporate ladder and become a CFO. But she's the first to acknowledge that as she progressed from auditor at Arthur Andersen, to manager at SBC Ameritech, to director of business development at Baxter International, to vice president at Pfizer, to treasurer and then controller at Visteon Corporation, she needed more than technical know-how to advance.

"Being technically competent and having the right credentials will open the door," she says. How you handle yourself, what kind of communication skills you possess, how much of a risk taker you are, will likely vault you into the corporate suite. That's what worked for Mary Winston, which helped differentiate her from her peers who were equally proficient technically and had an MBA.

Move Up One Rung at a Time

Winston has viewed her entire career as a continuum. One job serves as a stepping-stone to get her to the next job. That next job built her skills, expanded her repertoire, made her more marketable, and catapulted her to the next rung. "Every step prepares you for the next rung. People who move up to senior-level positions must continually raise the bar for themselves," says the African American native of Milwaukee, Wisconsin. Her audit job prepared her to become a manager in accounting, which led to her being named a director of business strategy, which enabled her to become a treasurer, which helped her become a controller and then CFO. She continually challenged herself, kept advancing, maintained superior performance, and worked on acquiring new skills in addition to ensuring her technical know-how.

Master Interpersonal Effectiveness

Despite her twenty-year career in finance, where people are known and rewarded for their skills in numbers and accounting, Winston also focused on mastering interpersonal effectiveness. And while many auditors and treasurers are technically proficient, she advanced beyond many of her peers because she added the interpersonal skills to her technical competence. She focused on being attuned to everyone in the company: her peers, her bosses, and senior managers. "For me it came to down to being aware of the unspoken cues that tell you what's really happening around you. This includes being aware of yourself, how you're perceived, how others are reacting to you, what others' motivations are, the relationships among others that could affect you," Winston says. In many ways, she showed the kind of skills that author Daniel Goleman discusses in his book *Emotional Intelligence*. Treating everyone—bosses, peers, and subordinates—with respect and maintaining positive relationships with everyone helped set the stage for Winston to advance.

Meet Senior Managers' Expectations

One quality that Winston possessed that helped her distinguish herself from her colleagues was her self-confidence. "If you have unwavering confidence in yourself, others will have confidence in you. There's an aura about you that you know what you're talking about," she asserts. That confidence leads to an ability to take risks. While many minority professionals reach a certain point and then sit back, Winston kept looking for the next challenge. "Once I master something, I'm ready for the next challenge. I don't like the status quo and prefer to try to make changes. Then I try to make an impact," she says. Her confidence enabled her to keep meeting new challenges: auditor, manager of accounting, VP, treasurer, controller, and CFO.

Build Your Skills and Overcome the Obstacles

When Winston was named vice president of finance and administration for Pfizer Inc., in Canada in 1998, she oversaw the finances of a $1 billion division. Since it was the Canadian subsidiary and situated away from headquarters, she could function independently. It was equivalent to running the finances of her own business.

Arriving at Pfizer in Toronto, Winston found herself in charge of thirteen subordinates. All were white Canadian men, and each thought that he should have been named vice president of finance, not Winston. "I was an African American woman, who was not Canadian, and they wanted to know why I was being sent there to be vice president of finance," she says. Their resentment was palpable. How was she able to overcome it? Her technical know-how played a role, since she proved to them that she was an expert in finance. She focused on answering their questions, which demonstrated her keen knowledge of taxes, financial reporting, budgeting, and cost accounting. She also made a special effort to be visible at meetings and off-sites throughout the company, going beyond her division.

Early on at Pfizer in Canada, she won her staff over. She told them at a meeting that she had been named VP of finance because corporate headquarters knew the staff in Toronto was top notch, which was true. She also enlisted them as partners in several projects. Getting them involved and getting their buy-in on key projects quickly defused whatever resentment they felt.

The quality Winston demonstrated at Pfizer, which has been essential to her advancing throughout her career, was her ability to consider what other people were feeling. In addition to possessing the superior technical competence of a finance VP and eventually a CFO, she had the interpersonal instincts to see what her subordinates and bosses were feeling. She could turn their negative feelings into a positive.

Leading her team and managing the finances of a $1 billion subsidiary prepared her for her next challenge when she was named treasurer in 2002 at Visteon Corporation. One job led to another; expanding her skills prepared her for the next job. Winston was always looking to stretch her talents, never resting on her laurels, and always open to taking risks.

Moving into the Corporate Suite

Visteon, a leading auto supply manufacturer, which generated $18 billion in business in 2004, promoted her to controller in 2003. She was externally focused and was responsible for investor relations, dealing with analysts, coordinating with bankers, raising funds, and liaising with the bond-rating companies.

Since Visteon, like several auto suppliers, was facing reduced income from leading U.S. auto manufacturers, it instituted a major cost-cutting initiative. As treasurer, Winston was placed in charge of a project team that was asked to reduce administrative overhead costs by $50 million. She energized a cross-functional team and instituted twenty-five major initiatives to cut costs, including outsourcing certain activities, renegotiating contracts with suppliers, and changing travel policy. Those cost-cutting measures resulted in a $90 million savings, nearly double what was requested. The project was highly visible, raised Winston's profile at Visteon, brought her recognition from the COO, and was even recognized by the Women's Venture Fund, a New York–based nonprofit organization that provides business loans and skills training. That project led to her promotion to controller.

As controller, her responsibilities were internally focused. She recorded the company's financial results and concentrated on ensuring that the company's operations were on course. Both jobs prepared her to become CFO, overseeing both internal and external finances.

Moreover, first as treasurer and then as controller, she became the public face of Visteon. "I needed to inspire confidence at executive levels. I'm the financial person in charge; people are looking to me for answers. I have to maximize financial performance," she says. When Scholastic was looking for a CFO, a premier search firm identified Winston as a candidate, and she earned that job in 2004.

Be Strategic to Overcome the Old Boys' Network

How did Winston overcome the old boys' network to advance up the corporate ladder? In her view, her success stemmed from building strong relationships. She didn't have to forge those on the golf course but was able to achieve that within the office setting. Her performance was superior, and she kept on challenging herself.

Be Mobile

Moreover, she, her husband, and her two children (aged five and nine) kept transplanting themselves, from Milwaukee, to Chicago, to New York, to Toronto, to Dearborn, Michigan, and back to New York. It helped that her husband is an engineering consultant, who travels on the job and could live anywhere. But Winston was ready to accept any challenge in any location, which expanded her skills. "I like change, and I'm flexible. If I weren't a risk taker and mobile, I wouldn't be where I am today," she said. Had Winston stayed with Arthur Andersen in Milwaukee, where she started, it is less likely she would have advanced so far.

What enabled Winston to become CFO of a leading children's publishing company and not be content to remain a vice president? Ultimately, a combination of factors converged to explain her success: superior performance, an uncanny ability to read people and forge positive relationships, self-confidence that can't be gleaned from reading a glib self-help book, superior intelligence, and the drive to succeed.

Winston's advancing from job to job, which enabled her to climb the corporate ladder, triggers the question Is there such a thing as loyalty in corporate America? Should you be changing jobs every two or three years to advance as Winston did? Or can you stay at one company for twenty-eight years as Al Zollar did at IBM, which didn't stymie him in any way?

My own view is that the days when most people stayed at one company for thirty-five years and received a Rolex (Timex?) watch upon retirement have faded. Most companies don't show loyalty, and downsize when earnings dip, so why should you? On the other hand, every career is unique, and it's hard to say absolutely that you should move. Still, most corporate employees are like professional baseball players and operate as free agents.

Anecdotally, after five to seven years at one company, you'll be able to ascertain if the growth opportunities are there. Zollar said that IBM was such a large company that he changed jobs several times in his career, kept moving up the ladder, and never had to change companies. Since he heads a $2 billion subsidiary, that worked for him. If you find yourself getting stale, sense that opportunities are not there for you, then it's time to consider making a move.

Every strategic blueprint is like a fingerprint or DNA and is unique to the minority professional. If you're getting complacent, consider a move. If you're thriving and advancing and are being groomed for a senior position, it may make sense to stay put.

Developing a Strategic Blueprint

In our introductory chapter, we suggested that early in your career you develop a strategic blueprint that will map your ascent through the corporation. Back in 1983, when Mary Winston earned her MBA from the University of Wisconsin and also become a CPA, she intended to become a CFO. In 2004, twenty-one years later, she reached her goal.

Before becoming CFO, Winston worked at five major companies, Arthur Andersen, SBC Ameritech, Baxter International, Pfizer, and Visteon. Each step Winston took up the ladder moved her closer to her target: becoming CFO. She knew she needed to expand her financial experience, become a manager, get involved in P&L, serve as controller and then treasurer in order to reach her goal.

At Arthur Andersen from 1983 to 1987, she started in the audit department, which usually gives an accounting professional a sense of how the entire company operates and how each business fits into the company's overall financial picture. It also trains someone in risks and controls, invaluable tools for a professional with managerial intentions.

Winston also knew she needed more experience and felt that serving as a controller would add to her tool kit and knowledge base. At SBC Ameritech from 1987 to 1991, she served as controller, managing staff in planning, accounting, and information systems. In this role, she was sharpening her managerial skills and expanding her financial responsibilities.

At Baxter International from 1991 to 1995, Winston served as director of the business development unit and also as international treasury manager. In those capacities, she was involved in a profit-

and-loss business and also oversaw marketing, customer relations, and product development. Moreover, she had to focus on short-term profits and long-term goals. All of these skills would prove useful when she was named a CFO.

Winston knew that in order to move up, she needed to head a major finance division. At Pfizer in Toronto from 1995 to 2002, she was vice president of finance for a $1 billion subsidiary. She was involved in all facets of finance for Pfizer's subsidiary, including planning, forecasting, taxes, payroll, and procurement.

Finally, Winston decided that in order to be named a CFO, she first had to become a treasurer. At Visteon from 2002 to 2004, she served as treasurer, overseeing its cash management, financial strategy, and risk management. That job also gave her external experience with investors, analysts, and bond-rating agencies, skills that would prove useful in her next role.

At the same time, Winston kept honing her communication skills. She led company meetings, spoke at external conferences, and networked within the company.

When Scholastic was looking for a CFO, it sought someone who had experience as a treasurer and controller, had strong financial skills, possessed a variegated managerial background, and was an effective communicator. Winston had the experience and credentials, and her communication skills came through loud and clear in the interview. She nailed the job, and has been CFO of Scholastic Inc., since 2004. Every job along the way, starting at Arthur Andersen in audit, moved her one step up the ladder, enabling her to reach her goal of CFO.

Sometimes You Don't Ascend in a
Straight Line

Mary Winston's rise up the corporate ladder was a straight ascent. Each job advanced her a notch up the corporate ladder. But often the movement upward can be gradual or circuitous, take a step back and advance a step forward. Johnny Taylor is the senior vice president of human resources for IAC/InterActive Corp, the cutting-edge Internet commerce conglomerate run by CEO Barry Diller. Since Taylor, who is based in New York, is an attorney who graduated from Drake University Law School, he has moved between two different worlds, human resources and legal, as he has climbed the corporate ladder.

Early in his career, Taylor was an attorney at the Blockbuster Entertainment Group. After four years there, he impressed his bosses and was named vice president of human resources, labor, and employee relations. That job interested him because he wanted to expand his business knowledge and wanted to run a business area, not just concentrate on legal issues. When Alamo Rent A Car made him an offer he couldn't refuse, he returned to legal circles and was hired as vice president of legal affairs for the auto rental company. Not enamored with working there, he left to become a senior vice president of HR at Paramount Parks. He was lured away to become president of HR Strategies Consulting at McGuireWoods, a major law firm. At McGuireWoods, he was instrumental in running the consulting arm of the law firm, which could tap his HR and legal expertise. That job intrigued him because he got to run a consulting arm and oversee its profit and loss.

But a funny thing happened at McGuireWoods. Taylor's job revolved around selling personal services, not products like at Blockbuster. The heavy emphasis was on selling, and in less than a year, Taylor learned that he didn't enjoy constantly selling personal services. He left and was hired by Lending Tree, a subsidiary of IAC. Unlike Winston's, Taylor's background jumps around from general counsel to HR director to at times doing both.

Become an Expert and Make Yourself Invaluable

Despite his moving between HR director and general counsel, Taylor attributes his rise in several corporations to two factors: becoming an expert and choosing the right mentor. When he was an attorney at Blockbuster, the company faced a major class-action suit. Working on that case, Taylor conducted intensive research and finally advised the company to pursue a middle ground that would satisfy the company's legal issues and business concerns. That response proved that he had understood the business and offered sagacious legal advice. That case, which was resolved as Taylor advised, raised his visibility and credibility in the company, and contributed to his being named vice president of HR, labor, and employee relations. "Make yourself invaluable in the company," he advises.

When he started out at Blockbuster, he very consciously scoured the company to select the right mentor for him. While other people interviewed for this book met their mentor through happenstance, Taylor's search was well thought out and calculated. "I literally scanned the organization for the right person," he acknowledges. He approached Tom Hawkins, who was an executive vice president and general counsel, and who was young, dynamic, and ambitious. Taylor was extremely straightforward, and said to him, "I want to progress within the organization, and think that I could learn the most from you." The fact that Hawkins was white and Taylor was African American didn't even enter the equation. Recognizing a common sensibility in Taylor, Hawkins served as his mentor, helping him navigate within the company.

Moving Beyond the Old Boys' Network

Street-smart and bright, Taylor recognizes that the old boys' network flourishes at many companies, which could easily leave him outside in the cold. But his attitude is that the old boys' network is like gravity. "Gravity exists, but we human beings find a way to stand up and overcome it. I know the old boys' network exists, but I want to defy it, find ways to beat it, and spend very little time thinking about it. Sort of like gravity," he says.

Furthermore, Taylor has learned not to personalize things in corporations. He notes that if other African American employees have difficulties with a majority counterpart, it could turn into a racial disagreement. He learned that "when someone doesn't like you, realize that it may have nothing to do with the fact that you're black. I don't like every black person." He's learned to forge positive relationships with many majority counterparts and avoid the ones with whom he doesn't click.

Understanding What Motivates Your Colleagues and Bosses

Taylor's rise up the corporation was attributable to his taking risks, his ability to execute tasks, his professionalism, and his outstanding performance, among many factors. But he also attributes it to his understanding the motivation of others. When he entered senior management, he started devoting considerable thought to understanding what motivates other senior managers as well as subordinates. "Some people are driven by money. Others by recognition. If you can figure out what their primary motivation is, you can make sure to reach them and get what you want from them," he says, without manipulating them. He learned to ask many of these questions from serving as HR director, whose role it was to figure out what motivates employees.

Raise Your Profile—Pursue Publicity

Johnny Taylor may not be a household name, but he has raised his profile in numerous ways. He volunteers as chairman of the Society for Human Resources Management (SHRM), the largest organization of HR professionals in the world with 207,000 global members. As chairman, he meets with senior government officials, HR thought leaders, and senior business executives. He speaks at conferences and has forged a national reputation because of this work. In addition, that role has led to his being interviewed by numerous media outlets including CNBC, Reuters, *Black Enterprise, HR Magazine, Time, Fortune,* and the *Wall Street Journal.* In addition to answering questions on HR issues, based on his legal background he's been interviewed on employment law, organized labor, and employment class-action litigation.

Taylor takes being interviewed very seriously. When a reporter calls to interview him on a topic, he will assign one of his administrative assistants to do a Google search on that topic. He will go home, study the background material, and to try to become extremely knowledgeable on the article's subject. "My goal is to become an instant expert and establish myself as a thought leader," he says. Taylor has also learned that publicity begets publicity. When *Ebony* named him one of its "Top Under 40 Business Leaders," it triggered considerable publicity. When *Fortune* interviewed him on how American corporations are betraying women, it produced several follow-up articles as well.

Developing a Personal Success Plan

Just as I advised you to develop your own strategic blueprint, Taylor has devised his own "personal strategy for success," he says. Just as companies engage in strategic reviews with short-term and long-term plans, he has done the same for himself. He reviews his past year, determines which goals were met and which weren't, and thinks about where he wants to be five years down the road.

Focus on Your Strengths

Jerri DeVard was named senior vice president for brand management and marketing communications at Verizon Communications in August 2005. Previously, she was chief marketing officer at Citigroup and also responsible for its e-consumer line of business. In order to advance into the corporate suite, she concentrated on "understanding what my expertise was." You must know "what you can bring to the organization, and you have to be good at partnering, since most decisions are shared." Along the way, she had to overcome other people's perceptions of what an African American woman could or could not do. "I think you're always up against people who don't think you can do the job," she reveals. But rather than becoming a "victim of other people's perceptions, I never defined myself by what others expected of me," she says. DeVard focused on becoming a brand-management expert and let her performance take her to the top.

When she was in the marketing department at Pillsbury, it was looking for ways to create buzz around the Doughboy, its symbol. Since the Doughboy's twenty-fifth anniversary was approaching, DeVard orchestrated a marketing campaign around that event. "We had zero budget and I had to convince each brand manager to provide funds for the campaign," she said. It was the biggest promotional campaign at Pillsbury until that point, was hugely successful, and contributed to DeVard's promotion.

Nor did she take golf lessons and try to become one of the guys. "That wouldn't work for me," she acknowledges. Instead, she again focused on doing the best job possible. Yet she admits that "it's not a level playing field and there is a deficit to overcome.

"There's no substitute for high performance. It's not enough though to be good. You have to build relationships of trust, develop people who want to be on your team," she says.

Moving Up from the VP Level

In DeVard's strategic career blueprint, she focused on "becoming passionate about something I'm good at." She loved marketing and did everything in her power to get involved in marketing projects that would be successful, dovetail with the company's goals, and play a critical role in the company's success. "Choose the culture and environment you can be successful in and then thrive in it," she says. Learn to overcome whatever objection confronts you, which can play out in a variety of ways. Take a lateral assignment; get another degree. Become an expert. "Plant your seed in fertile ground and know what you're best at doing," she advises.

Action Steps

- Use your new role as vice president as your launching pad. Now focus on establishing your reputation by helping your company boost revenue or extend its marketing, or using your ethnicity as a competitive edge.

- Determine what the dominant business initiative is at your company and get involved in it. Becoming a business leader is critical to your advancing.

- All companies want their senior executives to be leaders, but no one explains exactly what a leader does. Hence, it's up to you to define leadership at your company and then do something about it. Can you develop a task force, conjure up a new product, create a singular market plan different from what has been done before, or create a seminar for minority success? Think in ways that are different from what has been tried previously.

- Focus on your communication and intangible skills. By the time you've been named a vice president, most of your colleagues are technically proficient. You need to differentiate yourself by your superior communication skills. Become a leader at an industry group, become head of a volunteer group, or take the initiative at your company with a new venture.

- Don't let the old boys' network stymie your advance. If majority senior executives are spending one or two days a month at charity golf outings, see how you can get involved. Learn golf. If golf doesn't interest you, lead other volunteering groups in lieu of golf outings.

- Lead a major project team, just as Mary Winston did at Visteon, Johnny Taylor accomplished at Blockbuster, and Jerri DeVard achieved at Pillsbury. They built their reputation by leading major business initiatives, which ultimately catapulted them into the executive suite.

- Timing is everything. Getting to the executive suite means reading the corporate tea leaves. Anticipate what the next great corporate business initiative is, and stay one step ahead of it.

- Consider becoming a mobile executive. Though Al Zollar advanced his entire career through IBM, most people take the path of Winston and Taylor, moving from one company to another, changing locales, and building their résumé. Don't get stuck at one job and become paralyzed.

- Understand your senior managers' and colleagues' motivations. Taylor has delivered at several companies because he understood what motivated senior managers and peers.

- Court the media. Taylor has made a name for himself by his work at the Society for Human Resources Management and by delivering knockout interviews for newspaper reporters and TV journalists. He's been asked to write a book aimed at HR managers, which will only add to his public persona.

- If you find yourself getting stale or complacent, it may be time to make a move. Most senior managers profiled for this book changed jobs numerous times in order to advance.

- If the old boys' network operates at your company, acknowledge it and work around it. Form your own group. Invite like-minded people for an after-work drink or go bowling or play pool. Find simpatico executives who don't surround themselves with sycophants. Your network could consist of people of all colors, both genders, and all ethnic backgrounds; call it the rainbow network.

- Always adjust your strategic blueprint. What challenges do you need to get ahead? What skills are you lacking?

8

WHAT HR CAN DO TO LEVEL
THE PLAYING FIELD

■

IN THE EARLY 1990s, many corporations stepped up their minority recruiting. Top management was responding to a changing world, where markets were global and minority buying power was increasing. Human resources departments started recruiting at Historically Black Colleges and Universities and Hispanic-Serving Institutions and concentrated on urban colleges in Atlanta, New York, Washington, D.C., Miami, and San Antonio with large multicultural student populations. In fact, many American corporations did an effective job of diversifying their entry-level staff and bringing in thousands of talented minority professionals to boost their companies' ability to compete in a global economy.

But once the talented minority professional settled in at work, problems arose. The old boys' network often left the African American, Hispanic, Asian, American Indian, or ethnic employee excluded from many activities. Moreover, the tendency for majority managers to promote people in their own image kept the diversified staff from moving up the ranks. While companies devised effective recruitment strategies, many offered little help with assimilation. Once the minority professional arrived, he or she was often shut out of mentoring, both formal and informal, and denied mainstream networking opportunities. Since so many majority managers only promoted minorities to a certain level, many languished for years at a lower level. After five to seven years of stagnating, many left to open their own businesses, work for smaller businesses, or become consultants.

HR departments also feared that hiring a sizable number of minority professionals who might have to be dismissed later could trigger a series of lawsuits against them. Since many minority professionals were typically the last ones hired, they would often be the first ones dismissed. But if the hiring of minority professionals is done thoughtfully and strategically, in most cases class-action suits and sizable settlements can be avoided. The best way to avoid a lawsuit is to have a CEO who makes inclusion a major part of his or her strategic business initiative and creates a meritocracy throughout the company.

Nor are the federal agencies like the EEOC (Equal Employment Opportunity Commission) or the OFCCP (Office of Federal Contract Compliance Program) looking over the shoulder of most HR departments. While these agencies do ask for statistics on the ethnic and racial breakdown of staff, in most cases HR departments are able to make their numbers look impressive by adding mailroom clerks and administrative assistants. Most EEOC cases are triggered by an aggrieved person of color rather than by the agency taking a proactive approach and exploring why minorities have been shut out of executive positions.

Only high-profile cases with a smoking gun, such as the tape that revealed overt discrimination in a case against Texaco, have come back to haunt companies. Most companies recognize that if they hire minority professionals, they can promote or dismiss them based on the subjective criterion of performance.

Operate Strategically

Furthermore, most companies never thought strategically about developing top minority talent that could fill the executive suite. Most HR departments operate in a crisis environment. If a CIO resigns, the HR department goes into emergency mode. It contacts some executive search firms, reviews the company's internal organization to try to fill the slot, and considers the company's succession plan. But often the internal staff doesn't have the requisite background to fill the position. Rather than thinking strategically, the HR department rushes to fill one senior position without thinking of mandating a diverse slate. If a goal is to bring a more diverse slate into the company, HR quickly tries to identify a couple of minority candidates to fill EEOC requirements and then moves on to the next hire. The systemic approach to tactical staffing often excludes minority professionals from consideration for moving into the executive suite.

After the initial hiring, HR departments figure that attending one or two prominent minority conferences will solve their diversity recruiting. HR staffs of major corporations usually attend the National Black MBA conference and the National Society of Hispanic MBA conference in search of top performers to fill openings or for midlevel hires. Many firms consider these conferences to be the magic bullet of diversity staffing, which will solve their lack of finding minority executive talent and develop multicultural managers overnight. Ironically, most people circulating through the booths at these conferences are the active job seekers, who are typically the bottom-level candidates that can't find jobs, not the top talent who already have positions. HR staffers are able to find qualified candidates who have been downsized, often through no fault of their own. But the only top performers attending the conferences are likely to be speakers on panels.

Develop Relationships with Centers of Influence; Don't Look for Quick Fixes

To find top minority talent, my advice is to think strategically and build relationships with top minority talent, not see conferences as providing a panacea for identifying future middle- to senior-management needs. I refer to the strategy as "courting" talent. If you're going to attend the National Action Council on Minority Engineering (NACME) or the National Black MBA conference, identify two or three leaders of the organization. Invite them to lunch at the conference or to your offices if you're situated in the same city. Start building a relationship with these people who are centers of influence, which at the beginning won't necessarily involve asking if they have any suggestions for future middle- to senior-management talent. In the past, what HR departments did was attend these conferences, collect innumerable business cards and résumés (many of which weren't reviewed), and then call a senior executive with whom they had superficial contact.

Groom Minority Talent

In addition to courting minority talent, grooming outstanding minority professionals has been a problem at many companies. Many companies faced a difficult time dealing with outstanding minority performers such as Robert Charles, the Dartmouth undergraduate with the Harvard MBA, who was a senior executive at Ford Motor Company. Though clearly bright and the top performer in a Ford leadership program, he was hindered because he didn't play the game or become a yes man. Independent and forthright, he was dedicated to helping Ford succeed, which in his mind included questioning some of the strategies of his boss. While most of the yes men flourished and survived when a new CEO was named, he was asked to leave.

Did anyone outside of Charles's area nurture him? Groom him for a higher position? Note that he had outstanding credentials and was rated number one in a management-development program? Why was he left to sink or swim at the whim of his manager, who wasn't able to identify true leadership talent? What role did HR play? What role did Ford's diversity coordinator play? Why was he recruited so zealously, paid well, but then asked to pack his bags after less than three years? Where was the HR strategic succession plan? Was his boss evaluated on his ability to groom diverse talent?

At many companies, diversity programs are considered "flavor of the month" initiatives. Like comedian Rodney Dangerfield, they don't garner much respect. Just as total quality management programs were introduced with great fanfare and expectations in the early 1990s and vanished in the mid-1990s, diversity programs often enter with blaring trumpets and then fade when a new CEO is named. How does a company make its commitment to diversity part of the fabric of the company no matter who the CEO is?

Letting Everyone Rise to His or Her Maximum Potential

One company that made significant inroads into developing minorities and majority leaders was Chase Manhattan Bank, currently

JPMorgan Chase, under the leadership of Walter Shipley, its former CEO. Wesley, Brown & Bartle devised a distinct diversity strategic sourcing program to develop a pipeline of talent at the vice-president level, up through managing director, across multiple functions within the investment banking division. Since CEO Shipley was a major proponent of inclusion and diversity, the entire bank made a huge effort to groom and promote minority professionals. When Jamie Dimon was named president of JPMorgan Chase in 2005 and CEO in 2006, the emphasis on minority advancement cooled down. In fact, a reliable insider told me that before Dimon's hiring, there were forty-three minority managing directors at the firm, but that number dwindled to six under his leadership. CEOs can promote minority advancement or downplay it, depending on their vision.

This Chase talent acquisition program created a level playing field for all participants to maximize their talents. While minority employees were given no extra incentives, just the idea of having a level playing field meant that a larger percentage of minorities could advance at Chase. Unlike any kind of quota or affirmative-action program, minority professionals could move up based on their performance. The moral here is that if companies eliminated preferential treatment for majority candidates, minorities would move up the ladder based on their talents.

Build an Internal Pipeline

Another method that has proven successful for several companies is building a pipeline of talented minority performers. Before a specific job opens up, the company develops a succession plan that includes talented, skilled minority people in several divisions where it anticipates that senior managers will be needed. Then HR develops a plan to groom and nurture these minorities, providing them with the challenges and skills required of senior managers. Rather than waiting until the opening arises and then falling back on old ways of choosing majority managers, HR builds a framework in which talented minority professionals can grow into the job. That approach has proven successful at several companies.

Up until this chapter, the mistakes minority individuals make have been highlighted. Here are the top five mistakes that HR executives and top management make that result in minority talent leaving the company.

Mistake #1: Not Thinking Strategically

Too many companies operate in crisis mode, ignoring minority talent. Rather than thinking strategically about minority talent and using succession plans to build their current talent pool, they are constantly putting out fires. A senior executive leaves, and the HR department scrambles to call executive recruiting firms to look for talent, and perhaps requests that a diverse slate be presented. Instead I recommend building relationships with senior leaders of the Executive Leadership Council (ELC), the organization of 250 top African American corporate executives; the Hispanic Association of Corporate Responsibility; and the National Hispanic MBA Organization. Court them. Identify leaders and build relationships with them, and then you'll create a pipeline of talent for future minority leaders in your organization.

Mistake #2: Not Assimilating Your Minority Talent

Bringing in minorities to diversify your staff and increase the company's appeal to diverse markets makes good business sense. But it's not enough just to recruit and hire minority professionals; you must also lay the foundation to help them succeed. The sink-or-swim approach usually leads to most people of color departing the company after five years, when they see their majority counterparts advancing while they're stuck in place. Hence, what companies need to do is set the stage for minority professionals to succeed. That can be accomplished in a variety of ways through formal and informal programs.

Besides the formal mentoring programs that were mentioned in chapter 2, informal mentoring can lay the foundation for minorities to succeed. If HR has identified a skilled person of color as someone to develop, introducing her to strategic business leaders can play a huge role in her success. While majority candidates often enter with their own networks or can easily develop them informally, minority candidates need assistance in meeting the right people. Left to their own devices, they may often accomplish that on their own, but why leave it up to chance?

Mistake #3: Not Providing Support from the Top and Not Ensuring That the Plan Filters Down

Companies often create diversity committees, which strive to provide a level playing field, among other goals. But when you look beyond the frosting, you see a lack of substance on what diversity committees actually accomplish in terms of increasing the number of minorities in the corporate suite. At many companies, the senior management team is still less than 5 percent African American, 5 percent Hispanic, and 15 percent women.

In order to make a dent and have minorities operate on a level playing field, CEOs must serve as diversity champions. Not only must they must make it clear that senior executives will be judged on their ability to promote minorities, but executives' salaries and bonuses must be dependent on meeting those goals. If senior executives are not incentivized, there will be no teeth in the CEO's directives.

Moreover, many CEOs are proponents of diversifying their staff, but as the initiative moves down the managerial chain, the willingness to promote minorities gets undermined. In some cases, diversity efforts are given lip service, but since there's no accountability, those initiatives get swept under the corporate rug. Unless the CEO makes sure that each senior manager takes an active role in making promoting diversities a priority and is held accountable, it won't happen.

Mistake #4: Bringing in the Wrong Talent

Focused on improving their diversity numbers, many companies recruited minorities, beefed up their multicultural staff, and showed impressive improvement. In some cases, however, these new hires were set up to fail. Rather than concentrating on recruiting the best and brightest minorities, companies hired candidates based solely on skin color, gender, or ethnicity. While their numbers met EEOC guidelines, the minority professionals hired didn't have the right skills or talents to advance. Doomed to stay in their current job, they set a bad precedent, and many left. Progressive HR professionals acknowledge that it's not how many minority candidates are hired, but the quality of people that is paramount.

Mistake #5: Ignoring Early Intervention

After most new hires spend six months on the job, skilled HR professionals can usually determine which minority professionals are high performers, mediocre producers, or underperformers. Yet most HR people let staff sink or swim on their own. If someone has the right background, graduated from a top school and earned an MBA, and is still underperforming, there may be reasons why the employee and the culture don't mesh. Perhaps the minority performer requires a mentor to show him the ropes, or an informal network that provides feedback, or a change to another department, where he can flourish.

Since the minority professional is often on the outside looking in, early intervention creates an open dialogue with the employee that can help retain him. The HR representative can elicit how the minority employee is doing, what he would like to see happen that isn't, and how the company can better relate to the minority employee.

Early intervention can go a long way to providing course correction for the minority professional who may be having some adjustment difficulties fitting into a corporate environment. If majority employees worked at Black Entertainment Television or Johnson Publishing, which publishes *Ebony* and *Jet* magazines, and were surrounded by minority colleagues and minority senior managers, they too might face difficulties fitting in. Early intervention can be a way of reenergizing a minority professional.

What HR Has Done Well and What It Could Do Better

HR departments have done a commendable job of entry-level diversity recruitment. In fact, most companies at the lower levels are extremely diverse. But as many minority professionals' careers develop, something goes awry. While talented majority professionals get mentored and included in many networking activities, often the minority professional is on the outside looking in. Two changes need to happen to change the imbalance and level the playing field.

First, HR professionals need to nurture minority professionals and make sure that they have been given the same chance to succeed as their majority counterparts. Have they been given full access to mentoring programs? Is there something that HR could do to initiate informal networking? Are minority professionals given full opportunity to be selected for challenging assignments? Are minority professionals being groomed to move up just like their majority counterparts?

Are majority executives evaluated on their ability to develop a diverse staff? If senior executives are evaluated on their ability to identify talented minority managerial material, then minorities move up. If executives' performance appraisals and bonuses are based on their ability to level the playing field, results happen. On the other hand, if minority advancement is left to the good intentions of managers without any consequences or bite, it won't happen. When monetary incentives happen, results follow.

Three HR Approaches to Leveling the Playing Field

Rod McCowan, who is a forty-seven-year-old African American senior vice president of Global Human Resources at Hitachi Data Systems in Santa Clara, California, has both the pedigree and the experience of a leading HR executive. He has a master's degree in public policy from Harvard University and a master's degree in religion from the Yale University Divinity School, and he has served as a White House fellow in the first Bush administration and as assistant secretary for management at the U.S. Department of Education in the Clinton administration. Prior to joining Hitachi, he was also an HR director at a major furniture retailer and was managing director of the company's business in Asia, based in Singapore.

In his experience, companies at the executive level take one of three approaches to leveling the playing field:

1. CEOs and COOs at some companies have a personal orientation to do the right thing and recognize that their company requires a multicultural staff to stay competitive. With the backing of top management, "that senior HR executive can work to attract a diverse leadership team, which cascades throughout the organization to effect policy," McCowan states.

2. At some companies, the CEO and senior management team don't get it. These companies don't see any need to diversify their staff and don't anticipate that growing minority buying power will alter the company's revenue in

the future. "If the corner office doesn't want it to happen, there's nothing that can change that," McCowan offers.

3. Many companies find themselves caught in between these two poles: possessing a sympathetic CEO who likes the idea of having a diversified staff but doesn't make it the number one priority of the company. Without creating incentives, it's left to the senior managers to make hiring more minority senior managers happen, and often it gets put on the back burner.

Bring in the Best Possible Talent

In McCowan's experience, the most efficacious approach for the HR director to take to diversify the senior management team is to identify the most superior minority candidates, both within and outside the firm. If the HR director can uncover the best possible minority financial, marketing, or sales expert, then it increases the chances that the company will be open to hiring, retaining, and promoting her. Once that superior candidate is hired and succeeds at the job, it creates the positive momentum to recruit other talented minorities. The proof of hiring minorities lies in the success of each candidate. In a sense, each candidate's success breeds positive word of mouth throughout the company. "If you're an ambitious minority executive and aspire to the executive suite, you need to assess the competition and commit yourself to doing everything in your power to producing the best portfolio based on experience, knowledge, and skills that will ultimately position you to prevail," McCowan states clearly. It's the role of HR to identify the superior and outstanding minority candidates and then position them for promotion and success, based on their performance.

Nurture and Develop

Hiring the talented minority professional, McCowan emphasizes, serves as only the first step. The next step, which is key to retention, is for the HR director to nurture, develop, and help assimilate the new hire into the company. To hire talented minority professionals and let them flounder or thrive on their own is too risky. Once the minority executive is hired, McCowan arranges an accelerated learning curve. His goal is to make sure that the new hire is assimilated expeditiously into the culture and doesn't feel excluded, lost, or disconnected. Hence, he arranges meetings ("getting-to-know-you sessions," he calls them) with the new hire and the leadership team. He likes to create an open dialogue between the minority hire and the leadership team in order to get issues out on the table, clear the air, and establish communication, right from the outset. "Organizations are living organisms, which sometimes mean they can reject the outsider, especially a minority member," McCowan notes. These meet-and-greet sessions are a way to acculturate the minority member into becoming an accepted member of the team. They also work reciprocally, since the majority executive becomes more accustomed to the minority senior managers and feels more comfortable with them.

Coaching Recalcitrant Executives

If McCowan observes that any executives resist accepting new minority executives, he does not call immediate attention to the issue, as many HR directors do. While he avoids any kind of direct confrontation, he will directly communicate with the executive and coach him about the necessity of being open to new leadership team members. "I emphasize how working together is critical to the success of what we're trying to do here. I invite them to have an open dialogue to turn any negatives into positives. I encourage them to get to know each other better," he says. He stresses how teamwork will help the company achieve its goals and that partnering with the new executive will help both of them excel at their jobs.

At the same time, McCowan coaches the new recruit to communicate more effectively with the resistant executive. He points out that the majority executive hasn't been supportive and suggests ways that they can work together for common goals. He also indicates that the minority executive shouldn't take any resistance from other managers personally.

Focus on Making an Immediate Impact

Helping the new minority executives succeed isn't only about arranging meetings. McCowan helps arrange a game plan to produce concrete deliverables within one hundred days of the executive's being hired. Those concrete results demonstrate that the new minority executive is a major contributor and producer, a talented addition to the team, who can add value. Those actions will go a long way to dispelling any doubts that other majority executives might have about the person's capabilities.

What McCowan is doing is ensuring the success of the new hire and creating a positive environment in which the minority professional can flourish. Knowing that the new hire has only a limited time to make a positive impression, he coaches the minority hire, makes sure that results are delivered swiftly, and also coaches other executives who might doubt the newcomer. Further, by making sure the new hire succeeds at delivering a project early in his career, he's trying to establish a positive set of achievements to build on. In that respect, the HR director is playing a critical role in leveling the playing field. Of course, the onus is on the minority executive to make sure that his performance is outstanding and that everything the new hire does at the new company is exemplary.

Some Battles Can't Be Won

Prior to joining Hitachi, McCowan worked as a director of human resources for a major furniture retailer in the Midwest. The company was located away from any big city, in an area inhabited by few minorities. Nonetheless, McCowan tried to convince the company's CEO that because of changing demographics, a greater number of minority customers would be acquiring its furniture. Hence, diversifying the senior management team would make good business sense.

While McCowan was able to recruit some talented minorities at a mid-manager level, who ended up running some of the company's largest plants, he was never able to convince the CEO to bring minority talent in at a senior level. The company had operated with nearly exclusively majority management for many years, and most of its executives lived and worked in an area where few minorities resided. Most didn't quite understand what changing demographics meant. McCowan ultimately left to work at Hitachi, which was more open to recruiting and nurturing senior minority talent.

Introduce Minorities Through Internship Programs

Dave Edwards was a vice president in human resources at the Great Atlantic and Pacific Tea Company, the $10 billion supermarket chain first known as Family Mart and then known as A&P from 1979 through 2003. He is semiretired and lives in Greenville, South Carolina, but runs his own HR firm, DSL Consulting.

In the early 1990s, A&P wanted to broaden its talent pool at the senior executive level as a business imperative to help it appeal to its increasing number of minority customers. At that time, Edwards acknowledged that most majority senior managers at A&P had little exposure to minorities, so the company introduced INROADS (www.inroads.org), a nonprofit organization that brings in talented minority college students as interns.

Why use INROADS? "It was a tool to let mostly entry-level supervisors and middle managers see the best and brightest of students who had done well academically and were hungry to pursue a business career," Edwards says. Impressed by their academic prowess, hard work, and discipline, many supervisors forged strong working relationships with these INROADS students. In fact, Edwards says, about 30 percent of these students were hired full-time by A&P after they graduated from college. One important factor in the program's success was that managers and supervisors had "control over the hiring," he says. HR wasn't imposing or forcing them to hire anyone; it was performance driven.

"So much of this is about relationships that are color blind," Edwards explains. Ultimately, whether the INROADS student was from Malaysia, South Africa, or Ecuador didn't matter. What mattered was his or her performance and ability to help A&P reach its goals.

While at the beginning there was skepticism on the part of managers and supervisors concerning INROADS, eventually it was perceived as a positive addition that provided exceptional talent for the company. "It helped managers put a better team on the field. It made supervisors better," Edwards explains.

Increasing Access for Minority Candidates

In the early 1990s, when the Office of Federal Contract Compliance Programs started demanding that companies open up their hiring process and stop considering majority candidates only, affirmative-action pressure forced companies to hire more minorities. This pressure led to resentment from majority managers, who told Edwards, "I don't want to be an HR experiment." Many HR and line managers felt that that the company was relinquishing control over whom it could hire, and feared that minority candidates wouldn't meet the same criteria as majority ones. "In the early launches of these [affirmative-action] efforts, there were some failures," Edwards admits. Of course, if failures happened when majority candidates entered through the old boys' network, those failures weren't highlighted.

A&P decided to create a plan to hire more senior minority executives in a more strategic way. It brought in an executive search firm (Wesley, Brown & Bartle) to bring in mid- to senior-level talented minorities to meet senior executives, even though no new positions were open. "In that way, relationships began to occur, so when hiring opportunities came along, these people were considered," Edwards notes. In fact, Edwards recalls several situations where the minority candidate attended the same college as one of the senior managers.

The two alumni developed a relationship, which led to the minority candidate being hired when an opening occurred that fit his skills. This strategic approach—developing relationships with minority talent without interviewing them for a specific job opening—paid off. "It helped senior management get exposed to new talent," Edwards adds.

Leveling the playing field at most companies can occur in three distinct ways: (1) through osmosis, where minority candidates work their way up through the organization; (2) strategically, as it did at A&P, where the company tried to attract and hire more minorities to deal with a changing demographic; or (3) by government and contractual edicts, which often leads to conflict, Edwards says. This strategic approach gives the company more control over whom it hires and develops an external succession plan to be executed.

A&P wanted to hire more minority senior managers to "give it the competitive edge," Edwards says. "The more you can broaden where people come from, the better the probability you'll have talent from more sources and you'll have a more talented team." He likens HR managers to baseball general managers who brought in African American players and then Latino players to help strengthen their teams.

When any new senior manager was brought into A&P, majority or minority, problems could occur. The people who hired the senior manager would be delighted, but often many middle managers who were passed over were resentful and could be antagonistic. What should companies do to ensure a recruited senior manager's success? Edwards replies, "Provide earlier feedback on what's going well and what needs to be improved." If problems arise, the company can bring in executive coaches to help the senior manager adjust and assimilate in order to succeed.

Overcome Resistance

Despite the best efforts of A&P to recruit and develop talented minorities and increase the number of minority managers, many senior managers still resisted the idea. "They felt as if the company were narrowing the field to select the best candidate. They felt that this could put the company at risk," Edwards says. For leveling the playing field to be effective, senior managers must feel that the company is selecting the best possible controller, marketer, or sales leader for the job. In order for this to happen, it often requires a "leader who creates an environment where the whole group succeeds on a professional and interpersonal basis and where everyone moves toward the same target," Edwards explains.

Level the Playing Field Group by Group

Frequently when companies introduce cultural-change programs or more minority hiring, they do so company-wide. But when HR conducts surveys about such a program's effectiveness, some people will praise it and others will critique it. Edwards suggests that programs should be tailored to specific teams or groups. What works for finance may be different from what's effective for sales or operations. "Introduce the program work group by work group, plant by plant," and it will likely be more effective.

Hiring Minorities Helps a Company Win the War for Talent

"The companies who get diversity right as an employer will win the war for talent. The companies that find a way to create an open, participatory environment, where they can provide input of all God's creatures, will be the companies that win," notes S. Gary Snodgrass, an executive vice president and chief HR officer at the Exelon Corporation, a leading utility company based in Chicago, Illinois.

Companies are fighting battles to hire the "cream of the crop," explains Snodgrass. The corporations that are perceived as leveling the playing field, offering equal opportunity for advancement, and creating a welcoming environment will be the companies that minorities choose to work for. Other companies that lose the war for minority and female talent will become second rate. Snodgrass is suggesting that a company can seize the competitive edge by being a leader in promoting and nurturing diverse talent, which can increase its market share and help it appeal to its multicultural customer base.

Tracking Hiring

Creating that level playing field won't happen by good intentions alone. Ultimately, Snodgrass suggests, it happens when senior managers are held accountable for their hiring decisions. Exelon tracks the hiring of each manager and business unit. "We want our organization to reflect the availability of people of color and women. When openings occur, we insist upon a diversified slate of qualified women and minorities. It's not an afterthought; it's an insistence," Snodgrass declares.

Exelon has a formal business talent review, which tracks who is interviewed for each open position. If a senior manager informs HR that only majority staff is qualified for a manager's position, Snodgrass questions why that senior manager was unable to find any suitable minority talent to interview. If the senior manager says there weren't any available with the right skill set, Snodgrass will tell the person to "go back to the drawing board and return with a new slate of candidates." Hiring talent is one of the key drivers of Exelon's success, so Snodgrass takes interviewing a diverse slate of candidates very seriously. If Exelon has gaps in its minority talent, it focuses on developing them internally, staffing from the outside, or accelerating its pipeline of minority talent.

Moreover, senior managers are held accountable when minority professionals leave. "We review separation of all employees, particularly minorities and women who depart the corporation," he says. Senior managers will be questioned if large numbers of minorities and women are leaving the company. Issues of diverse hiring are brought into performance management, which affects promotions and salaries.

Helping New Hires Succeed

Once a new manager is hired, Exelon, like several companies, has an "on-boarding" program, which offers professional assistance on assimilating into the company. This practice is done for middle managers and above, both majority and minority. It provides internal resources, executive coaches, and sometimes both. It helps new recruits understand the culture and helps them be successful. Candidly,

Snodgrass admits that utility cultures can be "slow to move, paternalistic, hierarchical, and institutional," so knowing the land mines can be very helpful in succeeding.

Minority Managers as Role Models

Once minority managers are acclimated, Exelon wants them to be engaged within the company. Rather than setting themselves apart, the company encourages them to become internal mentors and coaches for other minority staff and to serve as role models. "We ask them to be visible and active," says Snodgrass.

Business imperatives have been driving Exelon's desire to level the playing field. Snodgrass explains that Exelon has a large number of diverse customers in two of its major markets, Chicago and Philadelphia, where its customer base is one-third white, one-third African American, and one-third Latino. "A more diversified workforce will help us better serve our communities, making for more satisfied customers," he says.

Sometimes it takes shaking up the culture to level the playing field. "You have to shake, rattle, and roll the culture to change it. Otherwise you have incremental gains. You need a business talent review process and to hold people accountable. If people don't get it, you need to replace them," Snodgrass asserts. In his eight years at Exelon, he says, about half the senior management team has turned over, and while that has happened for a number of reasons, those who couldn't adapt to a more diverse and performance-oriented culture were forced to leave. In order to win a competitive war for talent and create a level playing field, sometimes senior managers need to be replaced.

Building the Pipeline

Like many companies, Wyeth Pharmaceuticals is dedicated to diversifying its staff. "It gives us a richness of skills, expertise, and experience, which helps make us successful," explains Deborah Helmer, its vice president of R&D human resources, based in Collegeville, Pennsylvania. Ideally, she says, Wyeth's workforce should mirror its diverse client base. Furthermore, minority scientists and researchers will understand the cultural and medical needs of minority consumers, which could lead to developing new products to meet those customers' needs. But few minorities and women obtain doctorates in the sciences, a prerequisite for employment in most R&D positions, so identifying minority candidates is not easy.

In 2004, Wyeth R&D instituted Project Access, a partnership with Wesley, Brown & Bartle, the author's executive search firm, to identify mid- to senior-level Ph.D. and M.D. professionals, cutting across multiple therapeutic areas. The search firm had established relationships with minority medical and scientific associations, groups, and colleges that Wyeth did not, such as the National Medical Association, the Black Scientists Association, and the Association of Black Cardiologists. Wyeth described in detail what it expected from its ideal candidates. Project Access led to Wyeth's building a proprietary pipeline of approximately sixty minority Ph.D. and M.D. professionals. "Project Access brought in diverse professionals, whose experience and background are helping us round out our employee population and bring us closer to looking like our client base," Helmer notes.

Since many of these minority candidates were transferring from academia or government to the business world, Wyeth helped prepare potential employees for the transition. An HR representative and then a senior Ph.D. or medical doctor would contact them and fill them in on what to expect if they opted to make the transition. During the interview, Wyeth personnel asked "situational questions," presenting a scenario in which the candidate had to deal with a difficult employee, or asking for suggestions on boosting a team's productivity. The goal was to assess whether the candidate was prepared to make the transition to the business R&D world.

Nurturing Minority Talent

Wyeth R&D has also established a diversity-development program that lasts for one year, whose goal is to help minority talent succeed. The program targets high-performing, high-potential minority professionals, and provides a mentoring program, and quarterly learning and developmental activities that foster leadership. Mentoring is a key component of the program because minority scientists want to learn what it takes to rise up the corporation and learn what has worked for other professionals who have advanced. Networking with other minorities often proves equally beneficial in the program.

Development Plans Are Critical

Having worked on these diversity-development plans for several years now, Helmer has learned several key factors to helping minorities advance at Wyeth R&D. Devising substantive development plans has been an essential component. If minorities are informed of exactly what skills they need to learn and what behaviors they need to obtain or correct, it helps them know exactly what it will take to ascend to the next level. Without the detailed plan, it can be too over-whelming or too amorphous to figure out what skills are required. In addition, having regular dialogue with managers and having access to senior managers in leadership positions, often through informal networks, are other critical ingredients to helping minorities advance, she suggests.

Exposure to senior managers can mean the difference between advancing and stagnating. If a senior manager meets a certain minority professional, becomes familiar with her work, and is impressed with it, then when an opening arises, that person may be considered.

In fact, when Wyeth surveyed staff recently on workplace effectiveness, minority feedback revolved around wanting more access to promotional opportunities and increasing their exposure to senior managers.

Creating a level playing field for minorities to advance at Wyeth R&D—just as at other companies—is a very complicated activity. It requires the full endorsement and sponsorship of the leader in charge, senior managers being held responsible for diversity employment, and constant communication with minority professionals, Helmer suggests. Senior managers are evaluated on their "diversity awareness, diversity recruitment, and diversity retention," she adds. Nonetheless, Helmer would not offer any statistics on what percentage or increase of minority senior managers has taken place in the last few years.

Action Steps

Throughout this book I've been urging minority professionals to take control of their careers, become outstanding performers, outdo their competitors, and stay one step ahead of the company. Yet minority professionals can't operate in a vacuum or silo but need a level playing field to have an opportunity to advance. If promotions are based on going fishing with one's colleagues, and minorities aren't invited to the stream, there's little chance to advance. Here are suggestions for leveling the playing field, based on what some companies have done:

- Develop leadership programs based on performance that everyone has access to. Minority professionals don't want preferential treatment; they just want the same opportunity to succeed as their colleagues.

- Build internal pipelines where minority talent can be groomed and prosper. Since so many majority senior executives promote people who look, think, and act like them, minority professionals must be recruited and groomed in order to be given equal opportunity.

- CEOs must set the tone for minority advancement and make sure that senior managers below them are on board. Often the CEO is a diversity champion, but that message is subverted by middle managers who prefer the status quo.

- Once a minority professional is hired as a senior executive, surrounded by mostly majority executives, HR must create a program to ensure that he or she is nurtured. Sink or swim usually leads to drowning and the minority senior executive departing the company.

- Provide the minority senior executive with feedback. Often isolated as a minority executive, he or she must get the

same feedback that majority executives obtain. Encourage
it internally or from executive coaches.

- Encouraging minority interns demonstrates that diverse
college students can thrive in a corporate environment.
Programs like INROADS provide exposure to many
midlevel managers who aren't used to dealing with the
best and brightest of minority students. Since many
INROADS students become full-time employees, they
constitute a talent base for potential leaders.

- Increase the pipeline. Developing relationships with
minority students requires more than HR and
line managers attending one or two conferences. It
involves courting minority organizations, building
relationships with industry leaders, appearing at
conferences, and attending conferences of Historically
Black Colleges and Universities and Hispanic-Serving
Institutions.

- Hold senior managers responsible for interviewing a wide
range of candidates.

- Evaluate senior managers on their ability to diversify their
management staff and retain minority professionals. Once
senior managers feel the effects of their actions in their
pocketbook and bonuses, the number of diversity managers
often increases.

- Once minority senior managers succeed, set up a system
where they function as role models. Create panel
discussions with affinity groups; interview them for
internal publications; turn them into mentors.

- Provide greater access of minority professionals to senior managers. Often that exposure can lead to their being seen, noticed, and hired.

- Promoting minorities and creating a level playing field are part of a larger culture that is open to change, doesn't rely on the status quo, and can absorb new people into the culture.

GLOSSARY

∎

Insiders use a variety of terms that all diverse professionals should be familiar with. Knowing these terms can provide insight that can help overcome the hurdles that are sure to crop up in your climb up the corporate ladder. Here are some key terms discussed throughout the book.

Blockers and tacklers: Blockers and tacklers are senior managers who typically give lip service to diversity, say all the right things, and then promote only their colleagues and friends who look and think like them, undermining the company's goal of expanding into a wider array of executives. I advise you to identify who the blockers and tacklers are and then find diversity champions who can support your efforts to advance.

Branding yourself: Just as Donald Trump is known as a master wheeler-dealer and Martha Stewart is the queen of home entertainment, you can brand yourself in your company. Become known as the best operations guy, the marketing whiz, or the HR specialist who devises innovative solutions. That specialty can help you advance.

C-level executive: Your goal should be to move into the senior executive suite, or as Robert Charles describes it, to become a "C-level executive." He's referring to the litany of chiefs who are the company's senior executives: the chief executive officer, chief financial officer, chief marketing officer, chief diversity officer, etc.

Corporate tea leaves: Most corporate employees spend their days putting out fires, moving from one task to another and never thinking about their company's future and where the company is headed. But the strategic minority professional is constantly assessing where the company is directing its resources. If it's acquiring a company and changing its core business, that strategy should send a signal to the minority professional. Constantly assess how the company is changing, how your role is transformed due to this change, and where it positions you for the future.

Courting minority talent: Senior executives who want to ensure hiring a wide range of candidates must "court" minority talent by developing relationships with leading minority organizations such as the National Action Council on Minority Engineering and the National Black MBA Conference. HR executives can't simply attend an annual conference, distribute a couple of business cards, and expect that minority talent will flock through their doors. It takes time and building trust over the long haul.

Decoder ring: Much of what goes on in a corporation is done through subtext and innuendo, and is hidden beneath the surface. Just as in the film *Star Wars,* you need a "decoder ring" to figure out what is really going on. I usually recommend you tap your mentor and networking group to read between the lines. Is the company really devoted to diversity? Will it promote minorities? Is it interested in creating a level playing field? Often you need that decoder ring to find out.

Deselection: Because of Equal Employment Opportunity Commission rules, companies have to interview a wide range of candidates and not just majority men. But companies can hire whom they want. That's why companies often "deselect" diverse professionals based on their perceived weaknesses and limitations, often relying on hearsay from current and former employees. What you need to do is make sure you can meet all of their criteria based on performance, experience, and communication skills to avoid being excluded or ruled out.

Due diligence: Investment bankers and venture capitalists perform due diligence when they are considering acquiring a company. Due diligence involves doing extensive research. I recommend doing due diligence on a company that you are thinking of working for to make sure that it embraces people of color. Once you're hired, I also recommend conducting due diligence if you're thinking of transferring departments, to make sure that the hiring manager of the new department promotes minorities.

Five- to seven-year syndrome: For many minority professionals, reaching the fifth year working at many corporations involves facing the crossroads of their career. While many majority candidates use the old boys' network to make their connections and advance, many minority candidates are left behind. Despite being an outstanding performer and earning positive appraisals, the minority professional, stuck in his job and envious of his colleagues, thinks about leaving the company. The five-year point is the critical time of deciding whether to stay in your job and company or find new challenges. Of course, that opportunity can involve seeing how marketable your skills are or transferring to another division within your company.

Godfather or rabbi: Choosing the right mentor can be critical to your ascent. When Stan O'Neal at Merrill Lynch started advancing up the corporate ladder and gained the confidence of David Komansky, its then CEO, he selected the right godfather. Finding a senior executive who believes in your talent can serve as the most expeditious way of advancing.

Incentivize: If minorities are ever to be given the opportunity to perform on a level playing field, majority senior managers must be held accountable for giving everyone that opportunity. Diversity training and mission statements won't accomplish that. It will only happen when majority executives are incentivized with increases in salary and bonuses. Typically diversity works when it's tied to the pocketbook.

Nesting: Nesting may be beneficial for birds, but it is harmful to minority professionals. Nesting involves playing it safe, not taking any risks, and often staying in the same old job, without ever seeking out any new challenges. Most of the senior minority executives who advanced have not played it safe but assumed new roles, changed companies, and tackled new employment opportunities.

Old boys' network: Any time majority candidates are congregating, and minority professionals are not included, the old boys' network is operating. It can take place on the golf course, at the local watering hole, on a fishing or hunting expedition, or at a bowling alley. Rather than let the old boys' network doom your career, I advise counteracting it. Form your own "new person" network, which can include minority and majority colleagues. Strive to make your performance outstanding, add to your company's bottom-line results, and you'll overcome that network.

Oppression viewpoint: Some minority employees think that whenever something doesn't go their way, it's because corporations are out to get and belittle African Americans, Hispanics, Asians, or another ethnic group, or women. Let's face it, corporations have been charged with discriminatory conduct, but too often using the oppression viewpoint is an excuse to avoid taking responsibility. Don't blame anything on your being part of a minority group; instead, focus on finding solutions to your problems.

Political minefields: In playing corporate politics, you need to ascertain what the political minefields are and then avoid them. If you're working at the American International Group, and its former CEO has been forced out of the company because of ethical considerations, you won't bring him up at a meeting as an example of good corporate governance. Again, tap your mentors and informal networking group to determine what the corporate minefields are.

Possessing the whole package: In order to advance up the corporation, you need to make sure that your performance is superior, but you also need to look the part and act the part all the time. You need to exude confidence, possess a certain kind of presence when you enter a room, and never lose your composure.

Siloed: What invariably happens in many companies is minority professionals cluster together thinking that there is strength in numbers. Joining a minority affinity group is a positive, but spending all of your time with only people of your ethnic or racial background can be a deterrent. It can silo you off from networking and mentoring possibilities. Don't close yourself off to anyone; majority senior managers often serve as the best mentors for minority professionals.

Situational mentors: You can select a mentor for a specific project, task, or presentation. Not every mentor, whether formal or informal, has to stay with you on a sustained basis. If you're leading a panel at an external conference on a subject that isn't your specialty, you can select a situational mentor to help you with this one project and then move on.

Sponsorship: Al Zollar of IBM describes sponsorship as gaining the confidence of your manager and his or her boss. Turning your manager and senior executives into your allies is a key to moving up the corporate ladder.

Tissue rejection: Tissue rejection occurs when an organization embraces diversity, yet when the individual starts, the company isn't ready to embrace talented minorities. Rod McCowan says, "Organizations are like living organisms, which sometimes means they can reject the outsider, especially a minority member." Diversity is not yet part of the fabric of the organization.

Work the event: When it comes to networking, enthusiasm contributes to success. I've seen too many minority professionals who attend a professional conference with the same enthusiasm as going for a root canal. Don't see networking as a chore. Do your homework. Prepare for the event. Practice your four-sentence synopsis of who you are and what you do, without making it seem canned. And come to the event with energy, humor, and openness.